Dear Clayton & Kim,

I believe that God created families to teach us that True Love is sacrifice in the best interests of others. May you continue to grow in the Love that Christmas began!!

Love,
Aunt Judi

P.S. You can be a Crepen, too!!

My Most Wondermous Crepen

Blind Faith: Music to God's Ears

Judi Piscitello

WESTBOW
P R E S S®
A DIVISION OF THOMAS NELSON
& ZONDERVAN

Scripture taken from the Holy Bible, NEW INTERNATIONAL VERSION®.
Copyright © 1973, 1978, 1984, 2011 by Biblica, Inc. All rights reserved
worldwide. Used by permission. NEW INTERNATIONAL VERSION® and NIV®
are registered trademarks of Biblica, Inc. Use of either trademark for the offering
of goods or services requires the prior written consent of Biblica US, Inc.

Scripture taken from the King James Version of the Bible.

Scripture taken from the New King James Version. Copyright © 1979, 1980,
1982 by Thomas Nelson, Inc. Used by permission. All rights reserved.

This book is a work of non-fiction. Unless otherwise noted, the author
and the publisher make no explicit guarantees as to the accuracy of
the information contained in this book and in some cases, names of
people and places have been altered to protect their privacy.

WestBow Press books may be ordered through booksellers or by contacting:

WestBow Press
A Division of Thomas Nelson & Zondervan
1663 Liberty Drive
Bloomington, IN 47403
www.westbowpress.com
1 (866) 928-1240

Because of the dynamic nature of the Internet, any web addresses or
links contained in this book may have changed since publication and
may no longer be valid. The views expressed in this work are solely those
of the author and do not necessarily reflect the views of the publisher,
and the publisher hereby disclaims any responsibility for them.

Any people depicted in stock imagery provided by Thinkstock are models,
and such images are being used for illustrative purposes only.
Certain stock imagery © Thinkstock.

ISBN: 978-1-5127-5868-9 (sc)
ISBN: 978-1-5127-5869-6 (hc)
ISBN: 978-1-5127-5867-2 (e)

Library of Congress Control Number: 2016916362

Print information available on the last page.

WestBow Press rev. date: 11/18/2016

Blessed are those who have not seen and yet have believed.
—John 20:29 (NIV)

Reflections

Vision blurred through childhood
And taken much too early,
That other senses less deceived
Would sharpen, and with wisdom grow
As he grew tall and burly.

Deprived as well of Daddy's love,
Abandoned he, embittered.
Worldly fame and fortune sought
To buy his soul; it beckoned.

From rock 'n' roll to country and soul,
He sang and told a story,
But fame and fortune fleeting passed
So God would get the glory.

A deeper longing wrenched his heart,
A need beyond expression,
That naught on earth indeed could quench,
Nor could Eros lessen.

Heavenly Father, Creator, Savior,
Redeemer, Lord, and Friend,
Counselor, Intercessor, Empowerer, and Guide
Became his lifelong end.

With spiritual eyes he led the blind
To Christ, our Lord and King,
Who, giving Himself, He yielded to death,
Eternal life to bring!

Contents

For we live by faith, not by sight.
—2 Corinthians 5:7 (NIV)

Chapter 1

Tough & Tender Beginnings

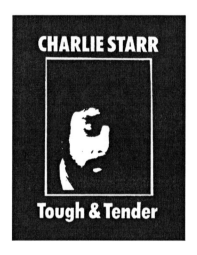

"For I know the plans I have for you," declares
The Lord, "plans to prosper you and not to harm
you, plans to give you hope and a future."
—Jeremiah 29:11 (NIV)

"My mother was from Naples, and my father was from Sicily. They met at a bank robbery," the burly, bearded musician joked with the rowdy crowd at Saratoga Performing Arts Center during the summer of '71.

"I'll kill 'em! I'll *kill* 'em!" he could almost hear his mother shout. He remembered the innumerable times she'd reacted with those exact words whenever he or one of his siblings had gotten into some mischief.

The heavy aroma of marijuana was billowing, and the audience was eager to hear Blood, Sweat & Tears, but there sat Charlie Starr, the opening act, perched confidently on the edge of a stool as he smiled wryly at hundreds of booing hippies who had already waited long enough.

The headliners' plane had been late, and the audience just wanted to cut to the chase. "We want Blood, Sweat and Tears! B, S, and T! B, S, and T!" they chanted in rhythm.

Over a loudspeaker, an overzealous announcer pleaded with the audience. "C'mon, folks! Let's welcome Charlie Starr! ... Let's hear it for *Charlie Starr!* ... C'mon, let's have a great big hand for *Charlie Starr!*"

The name was indelibly impressed upon our brains. For weeks after the concert, we joked, "Let's hear it for Charlie Starr!"

But there was no joking about Charlie Starr's talent. His powerful, gravelly voice cut through the announcer's feeble attempts to woo the booing audience, and he quieted the storm of anxious boomers like Jesus calmed the raging sea with a three-word command. Charlie's hard-driving and intricate guitar playing and his equally powerful piano style—along with his humor, wit, and warm charm—quickly captured the attention of those fickle folks who had initially rejected him, turning their boos into cheers in an unheard-of standing ovation!

It wasn't until he was *guided* back on stage that the audience learned Charlie was blind. Shrieks of surprise and delight along with thunderous applause accompanied his return performance, cementing into the hearts and minds of his audience Charlie's ability to overcome the "nothing thing" (Charlie's words) of his blindness with the many other gifts with which God had so richly blessed him.

This was my very first encounter with "my most wondermous crepen," a term of endearment that came about over twenty years later when God's perfect timing brought us together face-to-face.

But before I get ahead of myself, I'd like to allow Charlie to introduce himself in an essay he wrote on February 9, 1993, for a college English class.

> I came from a family of five children. My mother raised us on her own. My father left when I was very young, and I don't remember him ever as part of the family.
>
> One of the very nice memories from my childhood brings me back to the hot summer days in Buffalo when we were all home together. We'd play out of doors all day. Every now and then, my mom would come to the door and call to us, "If you kids are good, when the ice cream man comes we'll buy some ice—" The word *cream* was drowned out with our happy voices yelling and squealing.
>
> Then we would head out front at a dead run. We'd play for a while and then sit on the curb and just wait. Then finally, off in the distance, we'd hear the bell of the ice cream truck. "Ding-ding! Ding-ding!" it went, getting louder and louder as it came closer and closer.

Suddenly around the corner, the little truck would appear, the bell clanging to announce its cargo to the world. It was at that point that chaos broke loose on North Division Street!

Kids appeared from everywhere, it seemed, coming out of the houses, running from backyards—even coming from the next block over. We were all yelling excitedly.

Even the neighborhood dogs were running after us and barking. Then we ran out into the street, joined hands, and formed a chain of little kids that stretched from curb to curb. As the truck approached, we were jumping up and down, chirping out in our little six- and seven-year-old voices, "Stop! Stop! We want ice cream! We want ice cream!"

Our mothers then would appear and start yelling out our names to make us get out of the street and onto the sidewalk. The driver, amused but always patient (for this scene was repeated from neighborhood to neighborhood all summer long), then got out of his truck, walked to the back, and opened it up. There he would stand and hand out ice cream cones, ice cream sandwiches, and Dixie cups until everyone was served.

While we were hungrily devouring our little frozen treats, Mom would be scolding us for running out into the street. While she was trying to get our attention, we'd be poking and pushing each other, complaining, "He bit my ice cream!" or "So-and-so took too big of a lick!" or "She won't let me taste hers!" And then we'd all rush back into the yard and either dig up worms to put on our sisters' ice cream or resume whatever game we had been playing before all the ruckus began.

Mom would smile and kind of shake her head, turn, and go back into the house. All the while, we were totally oblivious to the fact that Mom always went without ice cream because she only had enough money for ours.

Recalling his third birthday party, Charlie—or Chuck as the family called him—described his memories of everyone gathered all around him as he was sitting at the kitchen table. His mother had placed in front of him a cupcake decorated with a lighted candle, along with a candy bar.

The candle made it easy for him to notice the cupcake. But when his mother urged him to look at his *other* birthday treat, he was unable to see anything else, as the color of the candy wrapper was so close to the color of the table. Coincidentally, the candy had been placed to the left of the cupcake, which happened to be in his "blind spot."

Frustrated with the unfruitful visual search, he resorted to feeling around on the table for the candy bar. At that point, his mother burst into tears. Having suspected for a while that there was something seriously wrong with Chuck's eyes, she finally had to admit to herself that she would have to take him to the doctor to evaluate the full extent of his visual impairment.

It was then that she learned he was legally blind, having cataracts and the beginning stages of glaucoma. At that time, there was no medication to reduce the eye pressure, and the cataracts were not yet operable. All they could do was wait and hope—and pray—that the pressure would remain stable.

A year later, as Chuck was wrestling with his brother on the bed, he didn't notice the nail sticking out of the headboard until it pierced his eye. Screaming in agony, Chuck ran to find his mother. Despite her desperate efforts to hold him tenderly and offer words of comfort, nothing could take away the pain.

In the emergency room, Chuck overheard the doctor tell his mother that the eye would have to come out. He cried out in desperation, "Don't take my eye! Don't take my eye! I'll be good, Mommy. *Pleeeease* don't let them take it out!"

Trying to soothe him, his mother said, "Oh, Chuckie, don't you worry. The doctors weren't talking about you, honey. They were talking about another little boy. The doctor is going to do an operation to see if he can fix your eye."

As they prepared him for surgery, one of the nurses approached Chuck with a mask. "Here, Charles. Smell the pretty flowers!" But the hissing sound and the pungent, sickening odor of ether coming from the mask were anything but pretty!

With all of his might, he wrestled and turned his head away from the mask and gasped for fresh air as they held his flailing arms and legs. But little Chuck was no match for them, and he quickly succumbed to the anesthesia.

When he awoke, he found that his hands were tied so that he wouldn't attempt to remove his IVs or the cone that had been placed over the gauze-filled gaping hole in the socket that once held his eye. His mother had lied to him, and so did the nurse.

Charlie later reflected on those tough and tender years of his childhood, mourning the loss of his eye as well as the loss of his trust in adults—especially those in the medical profession. Unfortunately, this was only the first of a long line of Charlie's encounters with doctors and nurses—sad circumstances and separations.

Charlie's father was never home. Some said he was a gambler, and many said he was a womanizer, but none of Charlie's siblings ever called him Dad. And that, indeed, was sad.

A few months later, Mom took Chuck for a ride to Batavia to visit "a special school for children who can't see." It was the New York State School for the Blind. They were given a tour of the school building, the boy's dormitory, the kindergarten building, the gymnasium building, and the shop where the older students made baskets and brooms, rubber mats, caned chairs, and all kinds of things out of wood.

They also visited the infirmary as well as the vegetable garden and the barn with the chickens and other farm animals. They were given a hearty lunch—complete with dessert—and Chuck even got to play on the playground with some of the other children while the adults talked.

"Well, Chuck, what do you think? Do you like it here?" asked his mom, hopeful that he had enjoyed his time at the school.

"Sure, Mommy! Can we come back again sometime?" replied Chuck, cheerfully.

Thankfully, little Chuck couldn't see the tears running down his mother's face, which was contorted as she attempted to conceal her pain. She didn't want to tell him that this was *his* new school and that he would be staying here but that she had to go home.

Of course she couldn't even think about telling him that she couldn't afford to visit him again until Christmas, when the school would send him home. It broke her heart that she couldn't even see her precious little boy for his fifth birthday in early December.

As Mom drove away, Chuck stood on the edge of the sidewalk crying, "Mommy, come back! Don't leave me! Come back, Mommy! MOMMY!"

Once again, Chuck's trust in his mother had been shattered, reminding him that she had lied to him about his eye. In his limited view (pun intended), he had been naughty for fighting with his brother and now he couldn't see like the other kids so his mother no longer wanted him. Chuck sobbed uncontrollably as the car quickly faded from view.

But Chuck was not allowed to grieve for long. A stout, stern matron grabbed his little hand and scolded, "That will be enough of that, young man!" as she dragged the weeping four-year-old to Hamilton Hall, the boys' dormitory.

In his new living quarters, the less than sympathetic matron busied herself unpacking Chuck's few belongings, leaving him to regain whatever composure a four-year-old could muster after being "abandoned" by his mother. After sitting on the bed for a while, trying to be quiet after being threatened by the matron, he slowly stood up and began exploring the room. On one of the dressers, Chuck found a toy car.

As Chuck played with the car, his new roommate came into the room. Seeing Chuck by *his* dresser, the little boy screamed, "Hey, you stole my car! Give it back!"

Hearing the altercation, the matron intervened. "Well, I see we have a little thief! Give that car back, young man! Just for that, there will be no dessert for you for dinner!" From that day on, whenever she referred to Chuck, she called him the "little thief."

The next morning, the menu for breakfast was oatmeal and prunes. Chuck could barely make out something dark in his bowl, and as he moved his face within inches of the bowl, he figured out that it was a prune.

Chuck liked oatmeal and he liked prunes, but he didn't like them together. As he was reaching into the bowl to take out one of the prunes, the matron slapped his hand. "Young man, you will use your *spoon!*" she demanded. Little Chuck did his best not to cry.

Not wanting to eat the prune with oatmeal all over it, yet not wanting to get into trouble for not using his spoon, Chuck just sat at the table while trying to figure out what to do.

The next thing he knew, the matron was placing his spoon into his hand, scooping out a prune dripping with oatmeal, and telling him to open his mouth. Chuck resisted, angry yet frightened.

The matron wrestled the food between Chuck's resistant lips and then held her hand over his mouth, telling him to swallow as she stroked his throat. Chuck gagged and twisted away, vomiting his breakfast onto the floor.

Infuriated, the matron immediately sought to find a mop and forced Chuck to clean up the mess. Needless to say, she was *not* Chuck's favorite person at the school, but thankfully she had been observed and within a few days of the event somehow vanished from the premises.

There were many things about the school for the blind that Chuck did like. He liked sending one of his little classmates up and down on the dormitory dumbwaiter that had been designed for laundry. He loved watching *Howdy Doody* on the television in Hamilton Hall, and he quickly fell in love with Princess Summer-Fall-Winter-Spring. He loved her so much that once he even licked the television screen! Thankfully, nobody was there to see him, but when Mr. Bluster tried to kidnap the princess, Chuck got so angry that he swatted his slipper at the screen and was sent to his room without breakfast.

Chuck also loved so many of the friends he made at the school—friendships that lasted throughout his lifetime; he kept in touch each June with students and staff members who attended the annual NYSSB Alumni weekends. The school was his home away from home, and they were his family. He appreciated all that they had taught him—not only the academics, orientation and mobility, and other daily living skills and social skills but also many other things about life that are the unwritten and woefully unsung benefits of attending a school for the blind.

Since his birthday was in December and he was big for his age, Chuck wasn't in kindergarten very long before he was moved from the kindergarten building into the big school building for first grade. His affections for the puppet princess thrust aside, Chuck soon fell in love with his first grade teacher. The contrast of her thick, long, black hair against her long, bright-yellow dress caught his good eye, and his heart just melted when it was his turn to sit in her lap as she read stories to the class. She was kind to Chuck and encouraged him when he did his work well. Of course, she was kind and encouraging to the other children, too, but Chuck just knew in his heart that *he* was her favorite!

One night, Chuck recalled being very tired and sick with a sore throat and a head cold. All this made him very homesick, especially for his mother, who—if he had been at home—would have made him chicken soup and tucked him into bed with a kiss and a little prayer. Yet he wouldn't be seeing his mother until Christmas, still many weeks away. He was also having a hard time breathing, which made it hard for him to get to sleep.

Chuck thought about how much he missed his mother. He remembered her prayers, which often started out, "Our Father," and since he didn't know his own father and he didn't know what else to do, he decided to pray. He asked Father God to help him get better because he didn't have his mommy there to take care of him when he was sick. Instinctively as he said amen, he opened his eyes, and there by his bedside was a blurry figure in white.

Frightened by the sight of this mysterious vision in his room, he quickly closed his eyes and pretended to be asleep. Then slowly he peeked and the figure had moved to the foot of the bed.

Chuck closed his eyes once again and silently prayed, "Jesus, thank You for sending an angel to watch over me." Then he drifted off to sleep.

The Christmas Village at the school for the blind was a local attraction for Batavia area residents. It was also the source of many a sweet holiday memory for students at the school.

That Christmas was a particularly lean year for Chuck's family. His mother had worked as hard as she could—in spite of her rheumatoid arthritis—scrubbing floors just to pay the rent and Chuck's hospital bills and put food on the table for herself and her children. She had just enough to spare for a candy bar, a new pair of socks, and an orange in each child's stocking. There was certainly no money for a Christmas tree, let alone a string of lights or decorations.

But that didn't stop Chuck's mom! She bundled up her little brood and took to the streets in the better neighborhoods surrounding the Bailey-Kensington projects, collecting cast-off Christmas tree boughs laid out for the trash.

Anna Piscitello and her little children took those unwanted trimmings back to their little home. There, Anna somehow found a way to attach them to the cabinet of the floor model radio to form a makeshift Christmas tree that her children would never forget!

They adorned the tree with snippets of tin foil twisted into icicles, cut-paper snowflakes and chains, and assorted decorations of paper plates and construction paper that they had made in school. Little Chuck was happy to be back with the family again because he was finally home from school for Christmas vacation!

Yet Christmas Eve, just like every other Christmas Eve that Chuck could remember, his mother just sat in her chair and cried, and cried, and cried—because one Christmas Eve years earlier, her own father had died in her arms. Each year her children would gather around her, hugging her and telling her not to cry, that her papa was in heaven and it was going to be okay. But when you lose someone you love so dearly, it will never be okay until you get to see him again in heaven.

Chapter 2

Cherished Childhood, Troubled Teens

Be strong and courageous. Do not be afraid or terrified
because of them, for the LORD your God goes with
you; He will never leave you nor forsake you.
—Deuteronomy 31:6 (NIV)

In spite of his blindness, or perhaps because of it, Charlie had
such a beautiful way of creating visual images with words!

Whenever he would tell a story, he painted such vivid images that you'd think he had been able to see clearly every minute detail of the scene. And when he was telling jokes, he often added dialects to make his characters come alive.

When he eventually became a pastor, Charlie put this gift to work to the glory of the God who had given it—the gift of making words come to life through the Word of Life, the Word that spoke the universe into existence! The name Piscitello in Italian means *fisherman*, and God had worked in Charlie to make him a *fisher of men*.

Charlie's gift of painting word pictures is evident in the following, another essay for his college English class. This one is dated March 22, 1993, and titled "Friendships."

> When I think about my childhood and the friendships that I've had throughout the years, I'm surprised that at fifty years of age the memories are so clear. They are clear not only in names but in the details of places and events.
>
> I grew up on North Division Street in Buffalo, New York. It certainly was one of the poor sections of town, but perhaps as God would have it, children are innocently unaware of such things.
>
> We lived in a small house that was actually in the backyard of a big apartment building. Behind our house was the playground of School #6, which was all fenced in so that no one could get into it without going through the school building.

There wasn't a blade of grass to be found anywhere—not even a straggly weed. All around the house was only dirt— deep, black, stony dirt. We would dig holes in it, pile it up, push it over, and throw it and never seem to get tired of it.

When I was three years old, it was discovered that I had some serious vision problems. Being a mom, my mother wouldn't let me play with the other boys. They had sticks and ball bats; they'd jump off the porch instead of using the stairs; they'd climb the trees and run out into the street after balls. Well, you get the picture. Mom didn't want me to get hurt, so I had to play with the girls.

My first really close friends until I was five years old were my cousin Mary, my cousin Lorrie, and two sisters, Becky and Pinky, from the upstairs apartment in our building. None of us ever knew Pinky's real name—not even Pinky. Mary was the oldest (almost five), so she was the leader of our little group, and we did whatever she said. My role was mostly to sit on the porch steps and wait for one of them to bring me her doll that needed to be spanked or held because it was sick or its "Mommy" had to go into the house for a minute.

Once in a while, Lorrie's dog, Blackie, would dart across the yard to chase down and kill a rat. We all shouted and clapped our hands until the excitement was over, then settled down to wait for the flies to come. And come they did, by the hundreds—by the thousands! It was always amazing to us that so many flies could fit on one rat. But there they were—it seemed like every fly in the world—until the cat would appear to drag the rat away.

At least once a day we would walk to the store on the corner—not often to buy something but just to do something. On the way, the neighbors would come out to see if we were okay and not misbehaving. Everybody watched out for everybody, and more kids would join the group until we'd all end up at the store. We didn't go in, but we would look through the windows.

A couple of times, Mr. Thompson even came out and gave us a bag of popcorn to share on our way home. Mary would take charge and make sure that everyone got some.

Ours was a multicultural neighborhood, but as children, we didn't know that. It just wasn't an important piece of knowledge to us. As children we simply didn't pay much attention to skin color or that someone else talked differently. And if we did happen to notice, it still didn't matter. Perhaps as God would have it, children on their own just don't seem to have prejudices against those who are different. Even though others may have perceived us as different from one another, we certainly didn't see each other as anything but friends. Gender, color, national origin, disability—none of these things interfered with our friendships.

Our parents, on the other hand, had one steadfast rule in our neighborhood. We couldn't play with the Puerto

Rican kids unless they put their clothes on. At home, the entire family—parents and kids—went naked, even on their front porch. But Mr. and Mrs. Sanchez, who could not speak any English at all, learned quickly to dress the children before sending them out to play.

I remember one time how our little group created quite a stir in the neighborhood. We wanted Marla and Elaina to come out and play, but their mother told us that they would not be out that day. Our little four- and five-year-old minds reasoned that they probably didn't have any clean clothes, so we decided to go to their house to play instead.

We went next door, got up onto the Sanchezes' porch, stripped off all our clothes, and knocked on the door. Imagine Mr. Sanchez's surprise when he opened the door to find five little naked bodies—three white, two black; four girls and one boy—wanting to visit his daughters! He started sputtering in Spanish, his wife got the hiccups, and the only words we could understand were "No, no, no!"

Mothers came quickly from every direction, scolding and pushing on shirts and shorts, and we couldn't for the life of us figure out what the big fuss was all about! Fifty years later, when I read the story "My Lucy Friend Who Smells Like Corn," by Sandra Cisneros, I was reminded that when I was a little guy growing up, I was fortunate to have had a few Lucys in my life. We may have been little, but our friendships were very big!

When I went away to school at age four, I finally was able to develop friendships with other boys. It felt good to play rough! The old cliché "Boys will be boys" certainly is true. We shoved and pushed and wrestled our way through grade school.

At the New York State School for the Blind at that time, the boys and girls were segregated, not just in separate living quarters but even in classrooms; and in the dining room, a half wall separated the genders. The boys couldn't play with the girls or even talk with them, which was very hard for me to understand, having spent most of my early childhood with girls. So for quite some time, the dormitory matrons thought I had a problem, and I couldn't understand what *their* problem was!

I was fourteen before I finally had what one could consider a best friend. In spite of the fact that our first encounter was a fistfight, or maybe because of it, Jim and I bonded almost immediately. From day 1, we were inseparable. Where you found one of us, you found the other. Even the dilemma of liking the same girl was easily resolved without damaging the relationship. I taught him to play the guitar and we started a band together. This lasted three years and then Jim moved out of state. We kept in touch for a while and still manage to contact each other every couple of years. But somehow I know that if we were to move close to one another again, we would pick up right where we left off over thirty years ago.

As I look back on my life, I've only had a few people that I could say were close or best friends. I was raised without a father and had to play with girls because my mother was overprotective, due to my blindness. With dormitory matrons and female teachers at school, I tend to relate best to women. Today my very best friend in the whole world is my wife, Judi. She, like my old schoolmarms, won't let me play with girls anymore, but this time I don't mind—because I do understand!

Because Charlie was only home from school for Christmas, Easter, and summer vacations, his childhood memories of his family were most precious to him. And he loved to share some of his favorite stories with others, sometimes embellishing them (just a smidge) to bring out the humor. Theirs was the typical Italian extended family with aunts, uncles, cousins, and grandparents living together or nearby. The women in the family would often gather to can tomatoes, make pasta, or cook birthday or holiday meals, and the children would "help" as much as little children are able without getting in the way or making a mess.

Charlie often told the story of a gathering that took place when he was too small to be of any real assistance. The women were making pasta, and there were noodles hanging on chairs, broomsticks, and curtain rods—wherever a noodle could be hung to dry. Charlie had been playing outside, and when he came back in, the women shooed him away.

So he went into the bedroom and jumped onto one of the beds, not knowing that it was the drying place for hundreds of homemade raviolis. Except for the ones that had stuck to Charlie's clothing, each individual pasta pillow immediately went flying in a different direction as little Charlie squealed and quickly jumped back off the bed, his backside covered with pasta and cheese.

"Chuckie, I told you to stay outside!" his mother bellowed as she hobbled as fast as her crippled legs could go to swat him with her cane.

"Anna, he's just a little boy. He couldn't see the pasta!" chided Aunt Rose, who was always protecting little Chuckie.

Aunt Rose's son, Chuck's cousin Johnny, was also partial to Chuck. Johnny once even took a beating that rightfully belonged to Chuck. The cousins later joked about it, but that little reluctant act of sacrifice was never forgotten, and from their teen years until Charlie's death, he was especially close to cousin Johnny. Like Frick and Frack, when Chuck was home from school, wherever you would find Chuck you'd find Johnny.

Another much remembered and joked about event in the family is when Chuck's brother (who shall remain nameless for reasons which shall soon become apparent) was getting ready to take a bath. The water was boiling on the stove, Chuck's sister Louise had taken her bath first (as always), and his brother was next.

As he was taking off his trousers, Chuck's brother leaned over to free his socked foot from the pant leg and he immediately became branded with the insignia on the hot stove. His wife has candidly testified that the brand was still legible!

Charlie would often remark that Louise was lucky to be a girl. Mama wouldn't allow the boys to hit a girl, so Louise usually got away with all kinds of tricks against her brothers. But one day, little Chuck had taken enough of Louise's teasing so he threw his glass eye at her.

"I'm gonna tell Ma, Chuckie!" Louise yelled at the top of her lungs as Chuck scrambled on the floor, groping quickly around to find the eye and put it back in before his mother found out.

Later that day, little Chuckie could no longer stand the pain. In his haste to put the prosthesis back in before he was found out, he didn't realize that it had shattered, and another emergency surgery was needed to remove the jagged pieces of glass from his eye socket. Chuck had learned a very tough lesson that day: not to hit a girl—with anything!

And then there was the time when one of his brothers (also to remain nameless) decided to wear a gas burner as a crown and got it stuck on his head so tightly that even olive oil mixed with bacon grease couldn't get it unstuck. Since Mom didn't have a car, she had to take him to the emergency room on the city bus.

Pushing him into a seat in the front of the bus, she quickly walked to the back so that no one would notice that he belonged to her. She then stared out the bus window as her little "grease king" son turned to her and cried, *"Maaa! Maaa,* it hurts!" Some passengers laughed hysterically while others, wide-eyed, covered their mouths, trying their best to appear sympathetic to the boy's plight.

Another story, embedded in Charlie's English paper titled "The View from My Window," told of an event Charlie would have been too young to remember firsthand. Instead he had heard it repeated by various older family members, each telling it from his or her unique perspective.

As family oral tradition revealed, the neighborhood kids had all gotten together and somehow convinced Charlie's brother Dominic to hang onto the clothesline that went from the third floor porches across the backyard between apartment buildings in the projects. Little Dominic giggled and laughed as they pulled him farther and farther out on the line.

But as he got closer and closer toward the middle, the line sagged and dragged and grew harder to pull. As Dominic began to cry, they tried to reach him from the ground, but none of the children was tall enough to reach him.

Thankfully for Dominic, Aunt Rose came to the rescue. Dominic was retrieved and, as Charlie's version related, "Everyone involved was administered his due recompense." The rest of the children went to bed that night without any dinner, except for "poor, little innocent Chuckie!"

For a week out of every summer for many years as a child, Charlie would go to Cradle Beach camp, along with other children with various disabilities. Although I can't recall whether Charlie ever revealed the boy's real name, Charlie occasionally mentioned his camp friend who had neither arms nor legs. The kids called him Bob because they would take turns throwing him into the pool and he would squeal with laughter as he would—well—*bob* in the water!

When Charlie was fourteen, he and some other children were playing ball with a baseball bat and a golf ball. Seeing the ball coming, he extended his hand to catch it, but it whizzed right between his thumb and index finger, terminating all remaining vision in what had been the good eye.

For a while, he thought he could still see, but he soon realized that his strong visual memory had taken over. Charlie held on to the damaged eye for many years, and to his visual memory throughout his lifetime.

Sometime in his twenties, Charlie had his guide dog, Princess, on a well-worn leather-like leash. Princess lunged and the leash snapped, flying upward and slicing Charlie's cornea so painfully that he finally agreed to enucleation. Somehow, Charlie believed, he was destined to be totally blind and that if he hadn't been blind he would have died much sooner, due to his fearlessly adventuresome and rebellious attitude when he was young.

Charlie recalled his family making wine and keeping a barrel of it in the basement. When Charlie's grandmother could no longer manage the stairs, she would send one of the children down to fetch some wine for the adults. Each time, she would insist that the child whistle all the way down and back to be certain they were not imbibing.

One day, Charlie was asked to fetch some wine, but he had a cracker in his hand and absent-mindedly popped it into his mouth before he remembered he was expected to whistle. Doing her best to ensure that Charlie wasn't drinking any of the wine, Grandma stood at the top of the stairs and called down in her broken Italian-style English, "I'm-a no hear you *wheessel!*"

Charlie's uncle, on the other hand, had rigged up a direct line to the wine barrel. He ran a narrow hose from the barrel out the basement window and up into his bedroom window, fastening the end of the hose to the headboard of his bed so that he didn't even have to get out of bed to have a little nip! It was even chilled a bit as it traveled outside in the winter!

Charlie learned the dangers of drinking alcohol early in his teen years. Having somehow obtained a cheap bottle of sweet wine, he and a friend quickly downed the entire bottle as if it were soda pop—only to get terribly sick by the time they made it back to the dorm.

The nurse in the infirmary was anything but sympathetic. Taking their temperature rectally "to see if it was something contagious," her sarcasm told them that she knew exactly why the boys were sick. And she made their stay in the infirmary as miserable as possible in order to ensure that they both had learned their lesson!

Unfortunately, however, Charlie did not learn the dangers of smoking until much later. His mother and many of the other adults in his family were smokers, and at that time, students at the school for the blind were allowed to smoke if they were at least fifteen years of age and had written permission from a parent.

Charlie's mother's signature was easy to counterfeit because she had a severe case of rheumatoid arthritis. As a result, her handwriting was large, shaky, and inconsistent. So Chuck was one of the "cool" guys who were allowed to smoke in designated areas outside, earning his cigarette money by selling rubber mats or brooms made in his shop class or using his "going home" bus money and then hitchhiking home.

Because Charlie had been sent away to school, he felt that his family had rejected him because he was blind. Not wanting anyone to see the pain that overflowed from deep within, he was particularly rebellious as a teenager, burying his feelings with attitude. He was the typical 1950s punk with slick-backed hair, rolled-up sleeves, jean cuffs, cleats on his shoes, and a mouth that—well, let's just say it got him into a heap of trouble.

His experiences in church during those teen years weren't of much help, as he viewed the priest as a cigar-smoking, womanizing gambler. He recalled one Sunday in particular, in which the priest announced a "silent offering" would be taken that day.

"You kids in the front with your pennies, we don't want 'em!" he growled. Later that day, Chuck had heard that his aunt had seen the priest going into a bar that was known for gambling. He also recalled hearing during his teen years that the priest felt it his duty to "take care of the widows" in ways the Good Book would definitely not support.

Charlie remembered his teen years at the New York State School for the Blind with mixed emotions. Smiling, he reminisced over ordering a large pepperoni pizza from Pontillo's Pizzeria and having it delivered by taxicab to the dorm for a grand total of a buck and a quarter, which included the cab fare and the tip! His first kiss took place on the school elevator, and his first fistfight was over another girl. More than one alumna from the school has since confided to me that she'd had a crush on him back then, especially when he played guitar and sang like Elvis in the school's dance band.

Charlie admitted sadly that he had insisted on being consistently and painfully rude to the teacher whom he secretly loved the most. This was something he later regretted as he reflected back on how much that must have hurt her, as she had tried her best to cut through his tough façade in order to bring out the potential she saw in him. Many years later, he even mentioned her in a sermon, likening her to God, who so deeply desires the best for us yet we continue to reject Him.

The school for the blind was built with Hamilton Hall (the boys' dorm) on the west side and the Park Lewis building (the girls' dorm) on the east side of the main school building. Both dormitories were connected to the school building with underground tunnels that had been built so that the children could travel between the dorms and the school without having to go outside in inclement weather.

Charlie recalled hanging out in the tunnels with his friends on occasion, once hiding some bottles of beer on top of one of the huge steam pipes in the tunnel. They returned later only to find that the bottles had burst, leaving an odor of stale beer in the tunnel for weeks afterward.

Charlie and his friends would often sneak out of the dorm windows (quite a distance from the ground) at night to meet up with the girls. They would then walk down the hill to the Northside Deli to buy a stick of pepperoni, a hard roll, and a cola, or they'd just hang out in the park across the street, naively assuming that no one from the school could see them—even in broad daylight.

Music was an important part of the curriculum at the school, and Charlie had already learned to play several instruments, including violin, trumpet, and piano. But what he really wanted to learn to play was the guitar, so that he could fulfill his dream of having his own rock 'n' roll band.

As luck would have it—or perhaps God might have arranged—Charlie happened to notice an old but functional guitar in a coal pile that was on the school grounds but off limits to students. Returning to the boys' dorm carrying a guitar with coal dust all over his clothes, he couldn't deny that he had entered the forbidden territory. Although grounded to his room, he was allowed to keep the guitar, so he used the opportunity to teach himself to play it.

He and his friends would often go to Roxy's music store and try out the instruments. Roxy Caccamise was a local and well-known accordionist. His patience with the students from the school for the blind through the years was to be greatly commended. Roxy's daughter, Rose, would often help out at the store, and to this day, she has taken on the family business, continuing in her father's loving, patient tradition as well as reflecting her heavenly Father's love toward everyone she meets.

So for some of the boys from what many in Batavia term "the blind school," the attention was on Roxy's instruments, while for others the focus was on Roxy's daughter. If the truth were told for Charlie, I think it was a bit of both.

Everyone liked Rose. Charlie reconnected with her when we moved back to Batavia as newlyweds, and she is still a sweet sister in the Lord to me even now.

Around 1958 or 1959, Charlie formed a dance band at the school for the blind with some of his classmates and instructors. They played not only at their own school but also at other area high schools (including my alma mater, Hamburg High) and even in a few clubs in the western New York area. Some of their songs were recorded at the school on heavy vinyl.

New York State School for the Blind dance band, 1959:
Arno Popp, Orlo Nichols, Edward Clute, Charlie Piscitello,
instructors (unknown), and Tony ("Pop") Cimino.

In 1961, Charlie yearned to graduate with his sighted peers in his home school in Buffalo. So he left the school for the blind and moved back home—only to find that Kensington High School was not prepared at that time to meet the special needs of students who were blind.

At that time, the only teachers of visually impaired students were employed at the state schools for the blind, so there was no one to order Charlie's books in braille. One would have thought that the high school would at least connect him with students who could read his textbooks to him, but Charlie complained that they simply placed him in his classes without any accommodations, hoping that he would absorb enough during class time to pass his exams.

By the time Charlie had determined that his school neither had the resources nor the desire to accommodate him, he had formed a rock band with handpicked Buffalo-area musicians, eventually known as Charlie Starr and the Allstars. His band was busy traveling all over western New York, so he simply quit high school altogether and earned his GED on the road while following his dream.

The following are excerpts from another of Charlie's college English class essays. This one, dated February 22, 1993, provides Charlie's perspective on one aspect of his teenage years.

> As I was growing up, I had an intense desire to be like everyone else. I didn't want to be different. Of course, being blind automatically made me different, but I denied the difference and treated my blindness as a mere nuisance. As I grew older, I developed a need to be an individual as well as seeing the importance of being an individual.

I did not want to associate with certain blind people because I was embarrassed by some of their mannerisms. I just didn't want anyone to know that I was blind— especially when I was fourteen. I just wanted to be "normal" like everyone else.

But it was at this very age that, because of my intense desire to be like everyone else, I was almost run over by a city bus, since I refused to carry a white cane. Hearing the bus coming but assuming that I had time to cross the street, I stepped into the street only to hear the screeching of brakes and the screaming of the bus driver, who came running out of the bus to shake me and ask what the ___ I was doing stepping out in front of a moving bus!

It was then that he noticed my eyes and realized that I was blind. That made me realize that it's safer for me that people *do* know that I can't see!

A sermonette that Charlie delivered on April 18, 1993, reveals Charlie's ability to use his blindness and his experiences as a rebellious teenager as powerful and effective teaching tools.

God has not only called Christians to be different from the rest of the world, He has commanded it. The English word *church* is translated from the Greek word *ecclesia* meaning "called-out ones." But along with our calling, He gives us the precious gift of His Holy Spirit, which helps us to be different. And He promises to reward us with eternal life with Him in His kingdom.

We all grow up wanting to be like everyone else. This desire is often strongest during our teen years, but it continues throughout our lives. I was no exception to these feelings when I was a teen, refusing to use a white cane because it would identify me as a blind person. It wasn't until I was almost run over by a city bus that I realized that identifying myself with that white cane could save my life.

White canes identify blind people. What identifies Christians? Our spiritual "white cane" that identifies us as Christians is a Christlike attitude toward others. In 2 Corinthians 6:17–18, we are called to:

> Come out from among them and be separate, says the Lord. Do not touch what is unclean, and I will receive you. I will be a Father to you, and you shall be My sons and daughters, says the Lord Almighty.

James 4:4 states that being a friend of the world is to be an enemy of God. God doesn't want us to isolate ourselves from the world itself, only the evil that is in the world. Romans 12:2 explains that we shouldn't be conformed to the evil ways of the world but transformed by the renewing of our minds.

Jesus said that people would recognize His disciples by their love for one another. Our attitude must be one of love, joy, peace, patience, kindness, goodness, faithfulness, gentleness, and self-control. These qualities make Christians stand out as different in a world in which most people care more about themselves than others.

Just as a white cane protects a person from danger, this loving, Christlike attitude protects us from sin. Most sin boils down to putting our own desires above those of someone else. If we are truly reflecting a Christlike attitude of love, caring for others more than ourselves, we are less likely to sin.

Most of us want to be like everyone else because there's a feeling of security in being identified as "one of the gang," with no risk perceived. Being identified with a white cane provides a different form of security.

But what greater honor is there than being identified with Jesus Christ, our Creator, Savior, Brother, and God? And what greater security is there than knowing that the Almighty God, our Father, is on our side, helping us to do our best and protecting us from harm, in supernatural ways, if need be? And what better reward is there for "daring to be different" than living forever as the sons and daughters of the Living God?

In another essay, dated February 22, 1993, Charlie spoke again about being different.

Individuality and developing a sense of self aren't just being different. Self-confidence and self worth must be tied to a person's ethics and personal belief system, but without self-righteousness and without arrogance. A person's individual belief system is a foundation upon which that person's life is built. Who we are is how we live, according to this foundation.

My studies are directing me toward a career in vocational rehabilitation services. My clients will be relying upon me for guidance and direction in their lives. My role model as a person with a disability is important. I must present myself to them as a knowledgeable, confident, positive, and principled individual, fostering my clients' own development of identity and independence as well as their productive integration within their communities.

Charlie's self-confidence and self-worth during his childhood and teen years had been a reflection of his feeling unloved and abandoned by his father from the beginning and abandoned by his mother because he was blind. Charlie, therefore, had developed a tough exterior in order to hide his pain and to protect himself from any future attachment to those who might reject and hurt him. But when he learned of the unconditional love of our heavenly Father, he embraced his value in the eyes of God. Based on the price Jesus paid on the cross for His eternal life, Charlie found his identity in Christ, and his earthly life took on new meaning and purpose. He became an advocate for and an example to people with disabilities, actively proclaiming—and living—the gospel of Christ Jesus.

Charlie had *felt* abandoned by his father and mother, unwanted, and unloved as a child. The truth, however, was that his mother loved him dearly and had no other choice when she sent him to the school for the blind. Yet Charlie didn't know this until he finally confronted her when he was fourteen years old. But perhaps because he had *felt* abandoned, unwanted, and unloved all those years, he later learned to deeply appreciate our heavenly Father's love and our need to love one another as Christ loves us.

Here is another of Charlie's English essays, dated April 8, 1993.

Love, in its many forms, is a subject about which probably more has been written than any other subject. From songs to books to poetry to research papers, love has been credited (or blamed) for igniting the full spectrum of emotions of which a human being is capable: joy, contentment, grief, jealousy, fear, depression, frustration, and elation, to name but a few.

Love is always hoped to be the source of happiness. However, I have found that the misunderstanding of what love truly is has more often proven to be the source of frustration and sorrow.

What is love? There are many definitions of and opinions about love: what it is and what it is not. *Webster's New Student Dictionary* provides several definitions of love, including "strong affections based on admiration or benevolence ... warm attachment, enthusiasm, or devotion."

Dictionary definitions cannot begin to scratch the surface of such a complex subject. However, we can use them as a beginning—a starting point on our way to understanding the true meaning of love.

There are also various kinds of love, which were given separate names by the Greeks and Romans. It is from many of their ancient writings that we in the Western world have derived most of our present-day ideas about our single English word *love*.

The Greek term, *philia*, is the base of *Philadelphia*, thus identified as "the city of brotherly love." Philia is the type of love one displays toward a sibling or dear friend. Philia implies a sharing of common bonds and is the basis of friendship, and it is just one type of love.

Our English word, *erotic* comes from the Greek root *eros*, defined in H. Norman Wright's book *Pillars of Marriage* as "love that seeks sexual expression." It is romantic, sensual love designed to bond marriages and create families. Yet acting on its own outside of the God-ordained bonds of marriage, eros is debased to lust. Far too often, this world mistakes lust for love, cheating us out of the most precious gift ever given.

Many have even gone as far as to change the marriage vows from "till death do us part" to "as long as our love shall last" with the values of respect, sacrifice, commitment, and true love falling as fatal victims in our throwaway society. Without these values, we set ourselves up to be ravished and then left to try to figure out what happened to us.

We can only live on the physical elation of the relationship (eros) for a relatively short time unless the other types of love are also present. We have all gone mad stumbling from bed to bed in hopes of obtaining love when true love cannot be taken: it can only be given. In fact, to take this one step further, it isn't *love* until you give it.

True love involves giving yourself over to the other person unconditionally for who they are (as opposed to what we want them to be). There is risk in giving yourself in love. You must be willing to expose your true self, and in so doing, you become vulnerable to the other person. Another part of the risk is change. Changing yourself requires putting the other person's needs ahead of your own. To be fair to the other person, you need to be honest about who you are and be willing to change for the benefit of the other person.

This does not mean that you must give up your own persona and become a doormat or an enabler. There are times when love must be tough. When my previous marriage fell apart, it was hard for me to understand why. Over a period of three or four years, I gradually began to understand why love sometimes has to be tough. I also began to realize that things happened the way they did because neither she nor I honestly knew what real *love* is all about.

Some of the barriers to maintaining a loving relationship include lack of commitment to and respect for the other person and dwelling on the negative rather than the positive aspects of the other person. We can only change ourselves, but it seems that we are forever trying to change the other person. It doesn't work.

When love is fresh and new, we tend to focus on the 80 percent of the person's characteristics that we consider positive, oblivious to the 20 percent that we could consider negative. As the relationship continues, we tend to focus more on the 20 percent negative characteristics than the 80 percent positive.

Oftentimes the very thing that attracted you to another person becomes the stumbling block that begins to tear apart the relationship. Most people have idealistic hopes for their love relationships, but when the other person comes up different from what we expected, we get angry and depressed that we didn't *get* what we *wanted*. Again, real *love* is not getting—it's giving.

It's time now to slow our lives down and recapture the values of commitment, honor, respect, kindness, caring, and generosity that we have so selfishly let slide. These are the qualities that work in developing loving relationships that last and are not easily shaken. True and enduring love is possible, if you are willing to take the risks of *giving* it.

Yet in order to love others as Christ loves us, we must realize that His love is supernatural, agapé love: the unconditional love of

God empowered by His Holy Spirit. Agapé love demonstrates our worth to God by His willing sacrifice and forgiveness, expressed by Jesus when He stretched His arms out on the cross to say, "I love you this much."

Chapter 3

"God Things"

And we know that in all things God works for the good of those
who love Him, who have been called according to His purpose.
—Romans 8:28 (NIV)

Perhaps you're wondering by now just what happened to Charlie
in those years from his teenage yearnings to become a rock 'n'
roller to when he actually became somewhat of a "rock Starr"
and eventually proclaimed his faith in Christ, "the Solid Rock,"

as a pastor. Well, again we'll hear Charlie's own words, spoken in his personal testimony, given in Rochester, New York, the week before he pastored his first worship service in our home in Batavia on January 31, 1998.

When I was growing up, and all through my young years, I always had negative experiences with men, beginning with my father—negative in the way that I was never shown any love from my father or from any other man. It just seemed that any man throughout my life that I got close to would either not turn out to be the sort of person that I would want to be with, or—for whatever reasons of their own—left my life. I never knew my dad—truly.

When I was very young—about three years old or even two—he left our house. My mom was stricken with rheumatoid arthritis very early in her life—at age seventeen. So for all of her adult life she was a very physically sick woman. Because my dad left, I never got to know him. I met him maybe three or four times in my entire life. If I added up all the time I spent with my father in my fifty-five years, it would probably be—at the outside—maybe fifteen minutes. Maybe.

I was brought up in a home in which my mom prayed a lot, and she encouraged us to pray. So very early in life, I learned about God, and I was excited about God—until I started going to church. Then I was given a "rule book" of don'ts—and if you do, you're going to go to hell and burn forever. And that's what I learned about religion. It was all don'ts, and if you strayed in any way whatsoever, you were going to burn.

Growing up in that church and its belief system, the emphasis was on the Virgin Mary, and when I was four years old, she was my first love. I was infatuated with the idea of God and Jesus, but as I grew and learned from the sources I was learning from, I began to doubt.

One of the greatest things I used to pray for was a father. And when I learned that I had a father in the Almighty God, things didn't look so good anymore. There were too many rules and regulations and no freedom or love. I started to feel this at age seven and eight years old.

My mother, who was in tremendous, horrible pain—it was an everyday occurrence when I was home—would cry out and scream because just turning over in bed was a major operation for her. She raised us from her bedside, not walking around and playing ball and going shopping with us. She raised us from her bedside; the control center of our house was her bed.

My mother used to curse God when she was in pain, crying out, "Why did You let me be born?" We would hug her and tell her, "Mom, it's going to be okay," and we held together as a family like that.

Then I became very angry with my father for not being there for us and for my mom. But as I grew into my teenage years, I had a girlfriend, and we became very good friends. And for the first year or so, we didn't even hold hands. It wasn't a romantic kind of relationship. It was just a really good friendship and we spent a lot of time together. And at fourteen, she was just someone I clung to.

One day we were talking and she opened up to me a lot of her life. She told me—not in these exact words—that she was a victim of incest, that from age eleven she had to be "submissive" to her father.

At first I didn't know what she meant. I know that's hard to believe, but I didn't have any idea what she was talking about at first. After a little more discussion, I figured it out and got very angry. I wanted to kill him and probably would have or could have if we were ever in the same room.

But then I transferred the anger to God. I thought about my life and my mom. When I was four years old, if you had any kind of disability whatsoever, you couldn't stay home. You had to go away to school. Well, you can't tell that to a four-year-old. I was sent away to the school for the blind in Batavia. I thought my family had given me away.

I got to visit my family for a week at Christmas, a week at Easter, and for the month of August. So I started hating my family, hating God, and I had a lot of hatred and bitterness in me for a long time.

When I was a teenager, you would not have wanted to stay in the same room with me. I was just miserably arrogant and sassy and know-it-all and pushy and had a dirty mouth. I just wanted to be like the world, and I was like the world. And I was miserable.

As I look back at my life now, I see how God had protected me and was very, very patient with me—and extremely gracious to me. I ended up in a situation that was very nice, by worldly standards. I was fortunate enough to be in the right place at the right time. Now that I know what I know, maybe even God orchestrated that. But I was able to pursue a very lucrative and successful musical career.

"here's Charlie

charlie is an artist

charlie is a talented artist

charlie is a talented blind artist

charlie is a talented blind artist who plays seven instruments

listen to charlie

listen to charlie and you will agree

charlie is a star

JUST PLAIN CHARLIE is—charlie starr"*

—From the cover of Charlie's album, *Just Plain Charlie*, Mercury Records, SR-61209, 1971.

Yet I got dumped into the middle of the biggest, vilest, evilest mess that you could ever imagine, with drugs and sex and other crazy, wild things. But do you know what? When I got there—what I'd been wanting all my life—I had such a fear of drugs and STDs that I never got involved with any of it. I never did drugs and didn't get involved in the wild orgies and things that I was witness to—because God was with me.

God had His hand on me! God put into my life a manager, John Perialas, who had a family at home and a wife that he was true to, and every time I went on the road, he was with me. So I got to hang around with him. We would go out to dinner or go for walks, and very few times did we ever have to attend any of those other things, with the exception of a few press parties and some other things that we really had to go to. But God placed this man in my life so that I had a positive influence, and I really didn't even understand that until much later.

After many years of being together, we had a few arguments about money, but other than that, my manager and I were good friends. Yet God began to pull a little harder at my heart, and I chose to follow Him and leave the rock 'n' roll world. That ended my close relationship with my manager.

During that time of transition, one of my friends got killed in a car accident on the way home from a concert. I went to his funeral and I started to think about some of the things Solomon had written about. What's life all about? What does God have to do with it?

You live your life, you do what you can, you build up a treasure, and then you die? What else is there? If you don't do everything right every second of your life, then you go to hell and burn. So why was I born? Then I remembered hearing my mother scream, "Why was I born?"

I turned on the radio one day and heard this radio evangelist say, "Why were you born? Do you know why you were born?"

And I said to myself, "No, I don't know why I was born, and I sure would like to know!" So I started studying the Bible.

That's another story about how I came to study the Bible. I started praying, and I still didn't know anything other than what I'd been taught as a child. I had never read the Bible, but I was in a desperate state of mind after my friend Nicky had died. I began to think of my own mortality and became very fearful of death. But I didn't want to live that way, so I started praying and praying.

One day I went into my room, closed the door, raised my hands, looked up to God, and said, "Father, do something with my life! I will give it to You. I promise You! I will give my life to You. Just do something with it! This is miserable living the way I'm living. There's no sense to life the way I know it! If You are there, if You are a real God, if You are my real Father, please, Abba, hear me!"

I shouted those words, and it didn't happen all of a sudden, but I'll tell you something that did happen. Within two days of praying that prayer, I opened my door to find three big boxes sitting on my porch, and they contained a complete eighteen-volume braille Bible.

I didn't ask anyone for that Bible. To my knowledge, nobody even knew that I wanted one. But God knew I needed it, and on the top of the box was a packing list that said it was a gift, prepaid. To this day, I don't know who sent that Bible, but I do know that God sent it. I just don't know who He used to send it to me.

I began reading that Bible, and I devoured it. Night and day and day and night I read it from cover to cover and listened to God. I began attending church and Bible studies and church conferences at every opportunity, and I brought my family with me, doing my best to be the kind of person, husband, and father that I thought God wanted me to be.

I haven't led a life—at times—that I am proud of. I've told you what I didn't do, but there are a lot of things I did do. But our God is a merciful, loving, and wonderful God. He's a forgiving God. He's our Father, and truly He's the only father I've ever really known.

I got to know Judi's father for a year before he died. He was a wonderful man, and I know for sure he loved and accepted me, and I was looking forward to many more years of growing that relationship. But he died.

I used to carry a lot of guilt about the way I brought up my children. I tried. I did the best with what I had, and now I know it was the wrong approach. I never had a father to pattern myself after in any given situation. I was on my own. I winged it and prayed a lot. I've apologized to my boys, and I pray they forgive me.

I know my Father in heaven has forgiven me, and I know that on the day that I gave my life to Him twenty-five years ago He had a plan to call me into the ministry. I know He placed me in His church for whatever reason He has in mind.

Next week we start the house church in Batavia, to make it a little closer for those who are now traveling either to Rochester or to Buffalo. I am thrilled that God has us involved in planting community churches to reach out, to evangelize, and to get involved in our communities.

Judi and I have been called to plant a church in Batavia, and I doubted for a while, but I said, "Father, I give my life to You, and I will do what You want me to do. Just help me straighten out my thoughts. Tell me why I'm here!"

Well, when God first told me—through His Spirit and from talking with our pastor—that we were being called to start a house church, I thought, *well now, wait a minute. That's not exactly what I meant. I don't mean to give my life to You that way!* But it's not a choice when God calls you, and Pastor Ken told me not to dig up in doubt what God plants in faith.

When I was on the road and God began to draw me to Him, I realized that I couldn't keep the Sabbath holy if I was working weekends. Yet when I began keeping the Sabbath, I did it because I had to—not because I wanted to—and I was angry about it. I resented God's calling me away from a career in which I was making $2,500 per day—and that was back in the 1970s.

Thankfully, I look at it much differently today, because when I cried out in desperation, "Abba, Father!" He answered me. Maybe not in the way I wanted Him to answer, but even when His answer was "Wait," He was answering me in my best interests. And He will answer you, too. He has promised never to leave or forsake us, and His word is true.

Well, that was Charlie's testimony twenty years ago. The little boy whose dad left him and whose family "gave him away" because he was blind actually began his music career at the tender age of eight. A yellowed clipping from the local newspaper tells of how Charlie appeared on a children's talent show on television in Buffalo. He told the emcee that he was saving his pennies to buy a violin so that he could take lessons at the New York State School for the Blind. Charlie sang "Lucky Old Sun" and returned to the school with his driver, Mrs. Lottie McCallum, a Red Cross Motor Service driver.

The next day, Mrs. McCallum received a number of calls from folks who had seen the broadcast and were offering Charlie their used violins. Others offered to contribute to a violin fund for him. Charlie kept in touch with Lottie for the rest of her life, long after she herself had become blind. Charlie's dear, sweet Lottie McCallum lived to a ripe old age of 101!

That article was among the first of many articles featuring Charlie in newspapers and magazines throughout his life. Many years later, Charlie would record "Lucky Old Sun" on one of his albums. At Charlie's son Dom's request, it was the first song played at Charlie's funeral in 2012.

A September 23, 1971, article in the *Village Voice* has a photo of one of his album covers, *Tough & Tender,* from Prophecy Records. The headline reads, "a first album is a prayer and a promise." How "prophetic" that Charlie's music career involved Prophecy Records and his later calling as a pastor began with a prayer and will end with a promise: fulfilled prophecy! Charlie will forever be known as a "lucky old son" of the Living God!

The *Village Voice* ad boasts about Charlie gaining a reputation in the country rock arena with his impressive guitar style and singing talent as the featured performer on Blood, Sweat & Tears' spring tour and summer concerts. This brief article in the *Village Voice* is followed by Charlie's September to October 1971 touring schedule with the Moody Blues.

Teen magazine's April 1972 issue featured a photo of Charlie Starr, referring to him as a "guitar and song virtuoso" ... "sort of 'mellowed Joe Cocker.'"

An August 1972 advertisement in the Hazelton, Pennsylvania, *Standard-Speaker* touts Charlie Starr as "showstopper of almost every major rock concert in the U.S.A. for the past 3 years," having "just returned from an extended appearance at the Troubadour in Hollywood, California." Later that year, Charlie was featured on tour in Europe with the British group Yes.

Charlie's recording reputation actually began to accelerate around the time he left the school for the blind when he began recording with Herb Abramson and Bobby Comstock. Five of Charlie's early songs are included in a compilation titled *That'll Flat ... Git It! Volume 4, Rockabilly from the Vaults of Festival Records*, which is available on CD from Bear Family Records. The songs are "Black Jack Joey," "'Till Time Stands Still," "Sick and Tired," "You Ain't My Number One," and "Christmas Twist." The CD enclosure reads, "In 1961, Charlie Starr was taking his best shot with rockabilly and nicely underproduced teen ballads." It is entirely possible that one or more of these songs were first recorded with Charlie's classmates and instructors on heavy vinyl at the school for the blind. (See photo on page 28.)

In addition to several unissued recordings and the singles "Good Morning, Freedom," "Memphis," "I'm Gonna Find a Cave," "Number One," "Solitary Woman," "Road Time," "Christmas Twist" (http://www.youtube.com/watch?v=GvVFmUIUix0), "Old American Dream" and "So Close to Heaven", Charlie recorded two albums: *Tough & Tender* and *Just Plain Charlie.*

On the cover of Charlie's *Tough & Tender* album, Tim Lane writes,

> Charlie is a man who believes in truth and people. Although he has been unable to see the world around him since he was eleven years old, he transmits through his music as well as his personality, sensitivity, insight, and a feeling for life that is enviable.

Indeed, Charlie's belief in and love for the truth and people, as well as his compassion, discernment, and zeal for life, were essential elements of his personality. These were also the character traits (spiritual gifts) that led him from his musical career to his career in counseling and advocacy and ultimately to his calling as a pastor.

One time, Charlie was backstage while preparing to go onstage at a concert and wondered out loud how many people might be there. Someone replied that this particular concert seated 11,000.

"Have you ever listened to 11,000 people?" Charlie reminisced. "I wandered out front before the show started and just listened. All those voices ... it sounded just like a huge waterfall. It reminded me of a description in the Bible, a passage comparing the sound of many voices to 'the rush of waters' ... it's true." Charlie smiled as he went back to tuning his guitar.

Charlie's heart for people was breaking as he pondered the percentage of performers who were involved with drugs. "It's no good. It doesn't help your work; it hurts. A performer high on drugs thinks he's giving the best performance of his life, but when he listens to the tape, he finds out that his work was bad, his timing was off ... I get a natural high from music. That's euphoria enough for me."

On the back cover of *Tough & Tender* is a quote from Millie Wilson.

He sees his guitar with his hands.
He feels his music with his soul
His hands on demand are just a blur,
Yet his eyes have never seen a blur
His music is a combination made up of one
And once begun you feel it fills your every vein,
Then when it ends you throb and ache and want to cry
And people stand to clap and cheer
But he only hears—that can't be true and sometimes
I think perhaps he sees more life than me.

Charlie's musical versatility was a product of his classical upbringing at the New York State School for the Blind combined with the encouragement of his instructors to also pursue his teenage interest in rock 'n roll styles like those of Elvis, Fats Domino, and Chuck Berry—as well as his love of country music, especially that of Chet Atkins. He also loved classic hymns and black gospel music and put his whole heart into playing it all!

An October 1972 article by Rick Wagner in the *Cornell Daily Sun* states,

> Last Friday, Bailey Hall was once again moved to the point of almost falling off its foundation. Charlie Starr and Blood, Sweat and Tears were responsible. Carrying an old Fender guitar, Starr got a full sound from just the electricity and his voice. With an incredible amount of feeling echoing from inside him, Starr sang the blues like not many can. After each number the audience responded with loud and well-deserved applause. Enjoying every second of his set, Starr's personality came across almost as well as his music. His mixture of country and blues was a welcome change from most first acts, setting a standard that BS&T couldn't quite reach.

The Milwaukee Journal, in its "Sounds of the Times" on August 4, 1971, featured Charlie's *Tough & Tender* album, which includes "That Lucky Old Sun"—the song he sang on the children's television show at age eight. The article notes that Charlie's music was strongly influenced by his contemporaries James Taylor, Carole King, and Richie Havens and credits James Taylor for giving Charlie his song "One Man Dog," in reference to Charlie's guide dog Princess.

A *Billboard* magazine article dated September 4, 1971 (page 36) headlined the Fifth Dimension and Charlie Starr at the Los Angeles Hollywood Bowl. The writer likened Charlie's voice to that of Joe Cocker, with his "raw, biting drive."

A second *Billboard* article, dated September 18, 1971, featured Charlie's twelve-city tour with the Moody Blues, highlighting his *Tough & Tender* album. *Billboard's* 1971 Christmas Day issue announced Keith Moon and Peter Townsend of the Who sitting in with Charlie at the Troubadour as well as Charlie's New Year's Eve opening at the Anaheim Convention Center for David Clayton Thomas's final performance with B, S & T.

In August 1971, Charlie played with the Fifth Dimension at the Hollywood Bowl, and in October, Charlie opened for the Moody Blues, playing at the Oakland Coliseum Arena. In December 1971, when Charlie opened for Blood, Sweat & Tears at the Anaheim Convention Center, newspapers all over the country were still talking about an October 1971 article in *Rolling Stone* that mentioned an incident in which Charlie had been arrested years earlier as a "peeping tom" near his home in Buffalo, while waiting on a street corner for his girlfriend. Charlie often joked about the teasing the arresting officer received from his cronies for arresting a blind guy as a peeping tom!

Charlie had also been arrested for driving without a license. He was driving a pickup truck going ten miles an hour in an A&P parking lot at 3 a.m. with a friend—just for fun!

When Charlie traveled by plane, he usually boarded early with his guide dog, Princess. Once (perhaps because he was with the Moody Blues) the pilot came back to meet him. He asked if he could do anything for Charlie, so Charlie asked the pilot to take the dog out one last time. Charlie then joked with the Moodys, imagining people in the airport pointing, puzzling, and laughing about a blind airline pilot!

In spite of being legally blind, Charlie never lost his ability to visualize people and their facial expressions. I believe that

God had given him a gift of discerning their hearts as well. He demonstrated a keen sense of tenderness toward those whose hearts were hurting in some way, and he went out of his way to do whatever he could to bring out the best in people, if only a smile.

From 1977–1979, Charlie served as a music instructor through the New York State Division of Youth at Camp Brace as well as at SUNY Oneonta, teaching chorus, guitar, and piano. Each of these programs was funded by a separate federal grant.

So just exactly how did Charlie happen to get connected with Blood, Sweat & Tears? The answer is simple! It happened just like things often do in an old movie!

Charlie and his manager, John Perialas, owner of Pyramid Sound in Ithaca, New York, just happened to be in the right office in the Big Apple when the Eagles' equipment truck broke down on the way to their gig as the opening act for Blood, Sweat & Tears. So as luck would have it—or was it another "God thing"?—the gig became his! When David Clayton Thomas heard the crowd's reaction to Charlie's talent, he literally picked Charlie up off of his feet in a bear hug, proclaiming, "I love ya, man!"

In the years that followed, Charlie traveled with Blood, Sweat & Tears, Yes (including a tour in Europe), the Moody Blues, the Carpenters, Johnny Cash & the Carter Family, as well as James, Livingston, and Kate Taylor, Billy Preston, Buddy Rich, the Fifth Dimension, Jerry Lewis, Charlie Daniels, Tina Turner, and many others. He even jammed with Elvis at Graceland, and when Elvis traveled through the Southern Tier, I am told that Elvis slept at Charlie's little farm in Coventryville, in Charlie's son Donny's bed—far from the paparazzi!

A September 2, 1992, headline in Rochester's *Democrat and Chronicle* reads, "Need for drug counselors strikes chord with musician." The article fills in a few more details about Charlie's convoluted career path up to the time we were first married.

"Charlie Piscitello is a man in tune with himself," the story begins. The article chronicles Charlie's life from his teens until that date. While in high school, Charlie had considered becoming a lawyer. But one day in the mid-1950s while he was rummaging around in a restricted area on the New York State School for the Blind campus, Charlie found an old guitar, and he was smitten with the "rock 'n' roll bug." He got caught and was grounded to his room for two weeks, allowed to leave his room only for classes and meals. Oddly enough, he was allowed to keep the guitar. Applying what he had learned from playing violin and piano, he quickly taught himself the basics of playing guitar, with the intention of forming his own rock band.

A few years later, a dance band was formed with classmates and instructors from the school for the blind. Playing a variety of '50s tunes (Charlie's young voice sounded a lot like Elvis), the band performed at high schools and mixed venues in and around Buffalo. They even recorded a few songs on heavy vinyl disks at the school.

Charlie often joked about one of his elderly female instructors trying to sing the Elvis Presley hit "Hound Dog" with a wobbly voice and proper English. "You aren't anything but a hound dog." The students rolled in laughter until their sides ached!

About three years later, Charlie began recruiting more seasoned musicians from the Buffalo area and the band began playing nightclubs in the city. Eventually, the band was dubbed

Charlie Starr and the Allstars, expanding the circuit throughout western New York and the Southern Tier.

Charlie had tried at first using his own name, but all too often his name was either misspelled or mispronounced (stuttering, stumbling, and stagnated after the first syllable) and usually brutally butchered. "Charlie Starr" was so much easier (and safer) to say than "Charlie Piscitello."

Those were some rough times, when Charlie played every gig he could find, and many times he literally sang for his supper. He admitted to being so hungry during those lean years that he often went fishing for his dinner, and once he was so hungry that he found it necessary to steal a chicken. But he never thought of giving up. Charlie Starr and the Allstars played together about nine years before they went their separate ways.

Charlie enjoyed playing high school and college concerts because he could feel the appreciation of those audiences. He especially liked the benefit concerts he played for "confined audiences," such as children who were crippled or those in penal institutions. These audiences genuinely loved the music and that was Charlie's compensation. He said it was "way better than money."

Charlie loved his music, he loved his fans, and he loved his family. Once he told a reporter that all the money he wanted was to buy his mother a house. Charlie really loved his mom.

Far from the college-bound potential lawyer he once dreamed of becoming, with the help of manager John Perialas, Charlie's path as a musician soon took him to bigger and bigger nightclubs in cities such as Boston, Chicago, Cleveland, and Detroit.

Eventually, Charlie Starr launched a solo career as a blues singer, writing some of his own songs as well as playing those of other performers. Charlie's album, *Just Plain Charlie,* took an unprecedented (and unrewarded) risk: rock music on one side and country on the other. In retrospect, Charlie admitted that the time just wasn't right for that.

Known for his raspy, gravelly voice and technical prowess on the guitar, Charlie traveled across the country with his guide dog, Princess. One student newspaper stated that Charlie always left his audiences "standing masses of goose pimples and tears." Another quoted Charlie chortling, "I want people to say, 'Wow, he's outasite! No pun intended!'"

Once at the Hollywood Bowl, when someone came to guide Charlie offstage after his set, a woman in the audience whispered, "Look! He's been arrested!"

By the time Charlie was recording his second album, *Tough & Tender,* James Taylor happened to be walking by the studio and came in because he liked what he was hearing of Charlie's music. James offered Charlie some of his own original songs, such as "Don't Talk Now" and "One Man Dog," that James hadn't yet recorded. Charlie then rearranged his album selections in order to incorporate James's songs. James sang backup on Charlie's album, and James and Carly Simon even joked with Charlie about getting married on Charlie's little farm in Coventryville.

Later that summer, Charlie got an unheard of three encores in Chicago and appeared on the Johnny Carson show. The fans loved Charlie, and *The Hollywood Reporter* and *Variety* raved about his performances. He was living the high life, meeting all the popular performers of his era.

Charlie had met Neil Diamond as a struggling songwriter, and encouraged him to sing his own songs. He met Mama Cass Elliot in the tropics when she was waiting tables by day and singing at night. The producer of Charlie's single "Old American Dream" was Albert Hammond, who sang "It Never Rains in Southern California."

Looking back on his life, Charlie felt that the Lord had been with him through it all, blessing and protecting him. Once while attempting to walk home with Princess in a snowstorm, Charlie found himself lost in a cemetery far from his home. Fearing for his life, he prayed, and when he reached out his hand, he miraculously found himself at the gate to his property.

But in the late 1970s, after playing thirty-nine gigs in a forty-two-night tour away from his family, Charlie had had enough of airplanes, tour buses, taxicabs, and hotel rooms. When he was busy doing studio work in New York City while opening for Yes on Rick Wakeman's farewell tour, most of his musical equipment, along with his suitcase containing all of his personal belongings, were stolen from a hotel, leaving him nothing but his guitar and the clothes on his back.

All those years on the road, surviving a rollover car accident, countless hard brakes and swerves, a few close calls, and several turbulent plane rides had left him more and more fearful of the travel that was an essential element of a rock musician's career. Every time he got into any moving vehicle, he said he just felt that he was "waiting for the crash."

When the ambulance driver arrived on the scene after Charlie's rollover car crash, he began shining a flashlight into Charlie's eyes, reporting, "No dilation!"

Charlie informed him that his eyes would not dilate because they were plastic.

The EMT replied, "Calm down, sir. You've been in a very serious car crash," thinking that Charlie had hit his head and wasn't thinking straight.

"No, you don't understand!" Charlie explained. "They're prosthetic eyes!"

But the EMT was too distracted to listen until Charlie popped his prostheses out and held out his hand with the prostheses staring up at the EMT. "Here! *Now* see if you can get these to dilate!"

Even after leaving his career as a traveling musician, Charlie's fear of travel eventually mushroomed into a fear of death that paralyzed Charlie, preventing him from venturing out of his home, fearful that whatever he did would lead to his demise. This went on for several months until one day his pastor asked if he would help deliver wood to a needy family to heat their home.

Charlie figured that if he was going to die, it might as well be in the process of helping out a brother, so he hopped onto the back of the truck. When they arrived at the church member's home, Charlie started heaving the wood off the pickup onto the friend's woodpile. He worked harder and harder and faster and faster as his fear of having a heart attack tried to grip him into stopping.

The more Charlie fought the fear, the more the Holy Spirit reminded him that God doesn't give us the spirit of fear but of power, love, and sound mind (2 Timothy 1:7). Although this revelation had broken Charlie's immobilizing fear of death, he never completely got over his fear of waiting for the crash every time he got into a vehicle.

Years later, even after we had been married almost 20 years, with his car seat slid forward, knees close to the dashboard as point of reference, Charlie had antacids in the car and another handful in his pocket whenever we had to travel anywhere. His fear of travel seemed to increase as he got older, so we rarely left Batavia, even to visit family in the Buffalo area, except when I coerced him to attend weddings and funerals.

Charlie Starr's finale in the music business was not so much due to his fear of travel but his faith in God and his obedience to God's call on Charlie's life, including his obedient refusal to work on the Sabbath. God soon whisked Charlie safely away from the "me generation" world of rampant "sex and drugs and rock 'n' roll" into His kingdom of love, wisdom, and power over sin. Charlie chose to obey God, leaving a lucrative career in this world for an eternal ministry serving the King of Kings and Lord of Lords!

Just when Charlie finally had the life he'd always dreamed of, God gave him a choice: fame and fortune for a season or abundant life with our heavenly Father forever. He made the right choice. It was a God thing!

But Charlie's choice to follow Christ—and the consequences that immediately followed—was far from easy. When Charlie gave up his musical career, his family very quickly began to feel the financial effects of his newfound faith.

Not only had he given up a very lucrative career, but he also had become part of a church that required him to give not one but *three* tithes. This included one tenth (tithe) of his earnings going to the church, saving another tenth for his family to attend church festivals in various locations three times a year, and every third year giving a third tithe to care for the widows, orphans, and other needy church members.

Although he tried his best to keep the family together, Charlie's first wife left him to finish raising the two younger boys on his own. Thankfully, he was able to fall back on skills he had learned at the New York State School for the Blind: tuning, repairing, regulating, and refinishing pianos and organs, in order to earn a meager living. However, sometimes Charlie found himself paying his driver (who also did some of the refinishing) more than he netted.

It was about this time, after the boys were grown and he had sold his farm in Coventryville and moved into an old trailer on a friend's dairy farm in Greene, New York, that Charlie's life would take another dramatic turn. Between the mysterious delivery of a braille Bible and the lure of radio evangelists, God began to give Charlie a reason to live.

While Charlie was on the road, he had observed the misery of those involved in drug and alcohol abuse, and although God had protected him from involving himself personally in drinking or drugs, he did have some very close friends whose substance abuse had cost them dearly, including his dear friend

Nicky, who died from an overdose. With the help of two of his pastors, who would often take him on counseling visits as a listening ear, Charlie began to gradually transition into the field of counseling. While tuning and rebuilding pianos to make a living, he began taking courses at Broome Community College, with the intention of becoming a substance abuse counselor.

Ten years later, after obtaining his bachelor's degree from Empire State College, Charlie had realized his niche as a counselor and advocate for people with disabilities, as well as his calling as an ordained pastor. While attending college and later working as a counselor at the Genesee Region Independent Living Center, he led a small Bible study group in our home. It consisted of individuals who attended the Buffalo and Rochester congregations of our church denomination.

As God was working to bring the denomination from cult status into mainstream Christianity (see *Transformed by Truth* by Joseph Tkach, Multnomah Publishers, Inc., ©1997), He was also preparing to call Charlie into the ministry. When our pastor, Ken Williams, asked Charlie to think about pastoring a church plant in Batavia, Charlie questioned his ability to serve God in such a capacity. As Charlie mentioned in his testimony, Pastor Ken's reply to Charlie was "Don't dig up in doubt what God has planted in faith."

The denomination sent us to headquarters in Pasadena, California, for pastoral training and ordination in 1997, and the group that had been our Bible study cell group became the core of the Batavia congregation, with our first worship service taking place in our home on January 31, 1998. The congregation was later chartered by the denomination in 2001, after receiving several awards for community service.

Once again, Charlie found himself featured in the local paper—this time in Batavia's *Daily News*. The headline read, "State Senate honors Rev. Piscitello."

> State Sen. Mary Lou Rath Tuesday named the Rev. Charles Piscitello as a recipient of the New York State Senate's first "Achievers Award." The award is intended to honor those who have contributed to their communities despite being faced with physical challenges.
>
> "This is quite an honor," said the Rev. Piscitello, who has been blind since he was 10 years old. "It's humbling."
>
> "The Achievers Award is an honor that recognizes the triumph of individuals over sometimes daunting obstacles, and is given to those whose efforts serve as an example of courage, personal excellence and achievement for our entire community," Rath said. "I am especially pleased to honor Pastor Piscitello because of his leadership in disability awareness and sensitivity issues."
>
> The Rev. Piscitello was nominated for the award by Ann Bell of Genesee Region Independent Living Center, where he was a counselor for five years, and by Stuart Steiner, president of Genesee Community College. In his nomination letter, Steiner said, "Even more significant than Charlie's professional and volunteer accomplishments is his untiring commitment to others and his positive,

upbeat approach to life. He is truly an inspiration to those around him and, without a doubt, he makes a profound impact on the lives of others."

Charles Piscitello grew up in Batavia. Early in life, he pursued several occupations, including carton construction, refrigeration, photo finishing, and operation of a magazine stand. In the late '70s, he repaired and tuned pianos. For a time, he served as musical instructor for the New York State Division for Youth and taught music at Oneonta State College.

An ordained minister, Piscitello is the founder and pastor of Batavia Christian Fellowship of the Worldwide Church of God and serves as president of the Genesee Council of Churches. As an adult, he obtained an associate's degree in human services from Genesee Community College and a bachelor's degree in human services and social work from Empire State College in 1994.

He has an extensive background in volunteer work, including hotline work as a Regional Action Phone specialist and co-hosting the March of Dimes Telethon in Buffalo, Binghamton, and Elmira.

The Rev. Piscitello is an accomplished musician, having taught himself to play guitar while attending the New York State School for the Blind. He eventually recorded two albums and toured with several performers, including Blood, Sweat, and Tears, Tina Turner, Johnny Cash, the

Carpenters, Mamas and Papas, Moody Blues and James Taylor.

The Rev. Piscitello is currently Student Support Coordinator for Students with Disabilities at Genesee Community College. "Charlie has even performed with Jerry Lewis and Charlie Daniels," said Rick Ensman, director of External Affairs at Genesee Community College.

"He truly is a wonderful person," Ensman said. "He's not only an advocate for people with disabilities, but he shares his time, skills and enthusiasm with everyone. Anyone who comes in contact with Charlie feels blessed."

The New York State Senate Achievers award will be presented each spring in conjunction with Legislative Disabilities Awareness Day. The Rev. Piscitello was unable to attend the ceremony in Albany, which was Tuesday. In his letter of appreciation, the Rev. Piscitello said a person doesn't really achieve much in life on his or her own without having a good support system. "I have truly been blessed with a most wonderful support system throughout my life—my family and friends, teachers and mentors, employers and colleagues—people who have cared, encouraged, supported and cheered me on to achieve the highest level of independence possible in overcoming life's challenges," he wrote. Among his supporters, he said, are his wife Judi, and guide dog Cory.

Embellished with the New York State seal and a scroll that proclaims, "Attitude Is the Real Disability," the 2002 New York State Senate Achievers' Award was presented to Charlie. The text of the award follows.

> Charles "Charlie" Piscitello is an outstanding citizen who happens to be blind. He grew up in Batavia, and while attending the New York State School for the Blind, he found an old guitar and taught himself to play. A talented singer and musician, he toured with such performers as Blood, Sweat, & Tears, Tina Turner and James Taylor, and recorded two albums.

> After years as a successful entertainer, Mr. Piscitello returned to college and earned two degrees in human services. Following an internship at the Genesee Region Independent Living Center in Batavia, he worked there as Public Relations Coordinator.

> He currently is Student Support Coordinator for people with disabilities at Genesee Community College. Mr. Piscitello frequently conducts workshops on disability awareness and sensitivity.

> An ordained minister, Mr. Piscitello is the founder and pastor of the Batavia Christian Fellowship of the Worldwide Church of God and serves as president of the Genesee Council of Churches United. His congregation, following his example, supports a food bank, which primarily serves people with disabilities.

Mr. Piscitello is married, the father of four sons, the grandfather of six, and is well known for his sense of humor. Overcoming physical challenges to excel in three careers—so far—Charlie Piscitello of Batavia exemplifies everything for which the Achievers' Award stands.

"Okay," you say, "so when and how did Judi finally meet Charlie?" Well, that, dear reader, truly was another God thing for which I am forever thankful!

When we finally met twenty years after I had first seen him on stage with Blood, Sweat & Tears, Charlie's boys were grown and he was living alone in a beat-up old trailer on an organic dairy farm, managing to eke out a meager living by tuning and repairing pianos. I had become certified as a teacher of the visually impaired (TVI) and was living in Churchville, just outside of Rochester, New York, having recently divorced a man who had given me a choice: him or the church.

I realized that no one but my Creator and Savior should be my God, and He remains my first priority according to my "life verse"—Matthew 6:33. I chose to trust that if God wanted me to be married, He would connect me with a man who put Jesus first and me second, and a year later He brought me to Charlie! It was a God thing!

One day a visitor came to the Rochester congregation I was attending from our sister congregation in Endicott. Crystal was hoping to attend a church wedding the next day and needed a place to stay, so I offered my apartment for her to spend the night. When she heard that I was a teacher of children who were blind, she began talking about her friend Charlie, who happened to be blind.

As she began describing his musical career and the bands he had traveled with, the cobwebs started to swirl in my brain, so I asked his last name. It didn't ring a bell. But then I asked if he had a different stage name, and when she said, "Charlie Starr," I could almost hear that crazy top-40-DJ-type announcer pleading, "Let's hear it for Charlie Starr!"

I laughed out loud to think that it might be the same Charlie Starr I had seen twenty years earlier! But I didn't think much more about it until the next evening, when Crystal invited me to visit her the following weekend and attend her church picnic.

She said that she couldn't really give me very good directions (she was the type of driver who would make an illegal U-turn on the New York State Thruway if she missed an exit), but her "friend Charlie" was great with directions. So she gave me his phone number—with a wink and a girlish giggle that revealed her blatantly Cupid-like intentions!

Charlie's directions were, indeed, flawless—especially considering the fact that he was blind and therefore had no visual memory of driving those roads. And his voice—believe it or not—sounded vaguely familiar, if only in my imagination. But I wasn't placing any bets on him being the same gravel-voiced charmer I'd seen twenty years prior until I could see him face-to-face!

When I arrived at Crystal's church, there he was, setting up the sound system for the worship service. He had cleaned up very nicely from a scruffy-bearded hippie to a clean-shaven gentleman in a three-piece suit. As I walked toward him, I took a chance that he was, indeed, the same Charlie.

"You must be Charlie," I said as he grinned, picked up his briefcase, and headed toward me.

"The old briefcase trick works every time," he later said, joking that he had run into me with his briefcase. We introduced ourselves to one another and learned that Crystal had invited us both, along with a handful of others, to her home for dinner after church.

Two of those invited for dinner were Barb and Sarah Simpson. Sarah was about eight years old at the time, and Charlie was like a favorite uncle to her. When Charlie invited me for a walk after the meal, Sarah tagged along, walking between us as if to protect "Uncle Charlie" from the big, bad newcomer.

"Charlie doesn't like fireplugs, you know," Sarah told me.

Charlie chuckled at my puzzled reaction. "Sarah, tell Judi what a fireplug is," he said as he grinned.

"It's a lady who's as fat as she is tall," Sarah replied, and the three of us burst into uncontrolled laughter. Our initial nervousness had been released like steam from a busted pressure-cooker valve. Sarah had quickly won my heart, and Charlie was gaining ground by the minute.

By the next day when we were at the picnic, I felt quite comfortable with the folks I had met at dinner, but the growing attraction between Charlie and me was unmistakably special. Charlie was the life of the party, and it was quite clear that everyone in the congregation loved him, and he loved them. Theirs was a lovingly tight-knit family, as the early church is portrayed in the book of Acts.

I stayed close to Charlie throughout the entire picnic. Despite his chiding that I was free to mingle and meet others, I told him quite honestly that I enjoyed being with him and was meeting lots of people through him that I would probably not have met otherwise.

When it was time for me to make that dreaded four-hour drive back to Churchville, I looked back at Charlie and saw him standing with his heart in his hand like a child who had just lost his puppy. Perhaps I was attributing my own sunken heart to him, but I am firmly convinced that the feelings were more than mutual. We were in love, and *that* was a God thing!

Chapter 4

"I Hope You Like Green!"

By wisdom a house is built, and through
understanding it is established.
—Proverbs 24:3 (NIV)

The next two weeks seemed torturously long. Although we had exchanged telephone numbers, in our brief weekend introduction

I had learned enough about Charlie to sense that he was the old-fashioned romantic who believed that the man should make the first move.

The suspense was agonizing but well worth the wait. He finally called and admitted that he had been as conflicted as I had been, wanting to call me but afraid that I really wasn't as interested in him as he had hoped.

Thankfully, he forced himself to take a leap of faith. That phone call was the first of many, causing our phone bills to rise to dangerously expensive levels. We joked that we could have rented an apartment for the cost of just one of our monthly phone bills!

That's when Charlie suggested that we try communicating as much as possible by mail instead. Sometimes he would write on raised-line writing paper, sometimes he would braille a letter or card, and other times he would send a cassette tape filled with conversation interspersed with music. I saved each and every precious one and cherish them now that he is with the Lord.

Here are excerpts from his first cassette-taped letter to me:

> Well, let's see. Where, where have I put that dictionary? Oh, here it is! Okay, let's see. Here it is! L, N, S, T. Here we are. T! T-A. T-I. Here we go. It's got to be right here, now. T-O, no. Tool, no. Tooth—no, toot … I seem to have run out of words! Where in the world am I ever going to find "tuit"? (Short country musical interlude, featuring a song with the lyrics "Love makes the world go 'round … God made love. I betcha He knew that He was on to something, so He made you.")

Hi, Judi. Just me, but I guess you already knew that! (Nervous laugh.) Listen, it was really nice talking to you last night. I wish that we could have talked a little longer, but we've got to watch our pennies. Thanks for sharing the call. I appreciate that, and I got to talk to you a little longer. But I guess we'll skirt around those little details with tape and letters, if you don't mind. I'd really like to talk with you more often anyway.

You can probably hear the sounds of the farm in the background—the chickens and the calves and the motors and engines. I'll try to talk over that, sitting in my little side room here in front of my mixing board that I like to play with. It's got a lot of little things on it—big things on it, too (nervous laugh)—but I just thought I'd sit here and talk to you for a while.

It's Friday evening just before Sabbath, around six o'clock. Tonight Frank and Francine are going over to their daughter's for dinner, so I'm just going to be kind of on the farm all by myself, so ...

Anyway, I used to have a house in a place called Coventryville. It's probably ten or twelve miles from here, and that's where I lived for probably fifteen years anyway. Then after I got my divorce, I stayed there with two of my boys for a couple of years and then Joe went with his mom and Angelo went out on his own. I stayed there about a year by myself in that great big eleven-room house ...

You can probably hear the calves out there, getting all excited. It's getting near time to feed them. But anyway, I stayed there by myself and I tried to sell it but I couldn't. I had ads in the paper and I had real estate people. I didn't sign any exclusives; I just had a lot of real estate people trying to sell it for me, but it just wouldn't go and it wouldn't go. Well, finally I closed the house down because it seemed I was over here at the farm more than I was at the house.

So Frank said, "Look, I've got a couple of rooms upstairs that I never use. Why don't you just bring a bed and come over and stay?" So I did; I came over and moved in. Things worked out fairly well. I lived there almost three years, and in those three years, there were never any harsh words between us.

Well, if you knew Frank and Francine, you'd understand that. They're just—you know, the kind of people that—just really loving and giving people. So you just try to do your best to be respectful of them.

It was ... it was, uh, different. It was a different kind of experience, living with another family. But I was kind of like an uncle to the kids and things just worked out.

Well, anyway, one of the hired men lived in this trailer and there was a house across from the farmhouse that another hired man lived in. When the guy in the house quit and moved out, the guy in the trailer moved into the house, so I asked Frank if he'd be willing to rent the trailer to me. Well, Frank wasn't sure the trailer was in any condition to be moved into, but we did a lot of cleaning. We cleaned for probably two weeks, scraping, scrubbing, washing, and painting. We finally got it all clean and I moved in.

It's good to have your own place, and I don't mean that in a negative way. I'm sure it was a relief to Frank and Francine to have their house and their privacy back without somebody else always being there. And as I said, I tried to be respectful of their time and their space, so here I am in my mobile home.

So anyway, I finally sold that house in Coventryville. But two weeks to the day after I signed the closing, they started putting up signs on the corner where I lived that they were going to put a nuclear waste dump in that area. And from that point on, real estate sales just stopped. Nobody still is buying anything because they haven't settled the issue yet. So if I had waited any longer, I would probably either still have the home, or—more likely—I would have lost it by now. Because business was really poor last year, so I don't know that I could have kept the place up. But the Lord worked all of that out, and here I am! (Short instrumental musical interlude.)

Oh, I had to quit for a few minutes there. Things were really building to a frenzy here! Frank and the boys made a canon out of an old pipe of some kind or other. They fill it up. I don't know if they use propane gas or acetylene, but they stuff it with tennis balls and old rags and set it off, and you should hear it! It makes a noise—well—just like a canon! It's really loud! The chickens go flying and clucking, the calves jump up and down, and the cows bellow! When you don't expect it, it really sneaks right up on you!

(Short instrumental interlude—fiddle music.)

Before I run out of tape here, I want to play you a song that Colleen Close and I are doing for special music tomorrow. It's called, "If We Only Have Love" and it's a revised version of a song by Shirley Bassey. I have a lot of Colleen's songs that we recorded together last summer, and I'd be glad to send you some more of them, if you like …

Well, Judi, I'm going to say good-bye for now and put this tape into a container that you can reuse. Just take the address label out and turn it over and it will come back to me just like a homing pigeon! Anyway, I enjoy doing this kind of thing, so I'll probably send you more.

I hope you have a very enjoyable rest of the week, and I hope to call you soon. Now, let's see if you recognize this sound. (Sound of key chain containing a metal round tuit engraved with Scripture.) Very good! We'll see you, Judi. Please keep me in your prayers, and I will keep you in mine.

The tape ends with a recording of Barry Manilow's song "One Voice," sung by the Young Ambassadors, a group of Ambassador College students.

Charlie sent his letters most often in braille or handwritten on raised-line paper. His handwriting was large, round, and scrawly, kind of like the handwriting of a small child, but it was legible, and I loved reading his letters.

The braille was more of a challenge for me to read because by that time I was no longer teaching braille to children but instead training teachers through the New York State Resource Center for Visually Impaired. As a result, my braille was beginning to get rusty.

It was actually my rusty braille that led to the title of this book. During our courtship, a group of brothers and sisters in Christ (brethren) from several upstate New York congregations got together and purchased an acoustic guitar for Charlie to play during our worship services. Naturally, they asked me to braille the card to accompany the gift. I guess my braille was okay throughout the body of the card, but in the closing my intention was to sign it, "From many brethren who love you." That's where my rusty braille went dyslexic.

In attempting to braille the word *brethren*, I inadvertently brailled a letter *c* instead of a *b,* as the letter *b* is formed by two dots oriented vertically whereas a letter *c* is two dots oriented horizontally. Likewise, in braille *th* is a contraction formed with a single dot in the top left and three dots oriented vertically on the right whereas a letter *p* in braille consists of three dots oriented vertically on the left and a single dot in the top right. So instead of brailling *brethren*, I brailled *crepren*, which later was shortened to become *crepen*.

As Charlie's creative mind played with the word *crepen*, he fancied that a crepen was a chubby little creature about three inches tall (much like a troll doll but without the hair). Charlie loved playing with his mixing board in his music room, and one day I received the most delightful tape with Charlie not only talking with a "crepen" but actually being entertained by a crepen playing a tuba—with his whole head in the mouthpiece and his tiny little legs dangling from it!

About a week after sending Charlie a package labeled, "TLC," that I had packed full of little surprises, I received another "crepen tape," this time with three crepens harmonizing to an original song titled, "TLC," in which the crepens thanked me for the TLC package!

Unlike the delightful little "crepen tapes," a few of our long-distance communications did not bring immediate smiles. For example, on one occasion, I received a two-page raised-line letter from Charlie. Unfortunately, however, he had inadvertently chosen a pen that had run out of ink, so there were two blank pages in the envelope! I called and told him that I was thankful he was a heavy-handed writer because I was able to decipher most of the letter by reading the indentations!

So to make it up to me, Charlie checked with Francine to make sure the pen had ink before writing his next letter to me. At the bottom of the letter, he included a Scripture reference.

He had *intended* to write, "Proverbs 24:3," which says, "Through wisdom a house is built, and by understanding it is established." However, somehow Charlie's brain short-circuited and instead he wrote, "Proverbs 23:3."

Again I called him, this time to ask the meaning of the Scripture reference. He quickly explained that He wanted to be certain that our marriage was founded upon Christ and godly wisdom.

"But Charlie, that's not what it says!" I said as tenderly as I could.

"What version are you reading?" he asked.

"King James," I replied.

"Just read it to me," said Charlie.

"This is what it says: 'Be not desirous of his dainties: for they are deceitful meat.'"

We both burst into uncontrolled laughter, and Charlie vowed never to make *that* mistake again! Needless to say, this was one story Charlie told over and over again, including a little speech at our wedding reception!

On still another occasion, I received a letter from Charlie that began by saying that he was having second thoughts about me. Here's what it said:

> Now, Judi, you know I love you. To my dear Judith Ann, if you could try to understand some of these feelings that I'm having—hopefully you'll be able to get to know me a bit and actually discover a greater insight into some of my thought patterns. Crazy as they are, you really should know about them.

> So let me start now. Judi, lately I've been having second thoughts about the wedding and marriage and about you as well.

Not having heard Collin Raye's song titled "Every Second," which had inspired this letter, I quickly jumped to conclusions and called him, crying so hard that I couldn't see to finish reading the letter! After he laughed at my naïve but premature reaction, he simply sang the song's chorus.

"Every second, every minute, every hour of every day,
Every second there's a thought of you that comes my way.
So if you ask that I've had second thoughts, I'd have to say,
Every second, every minute, every hour of every day."

After I collected my crazy emotions, he encouraged me to continue reading the rest of the letter.

You see, when we first met, my thoughts were daily. But they quickly became hourly thoughts. Then they shifted to minute-by-minute thoughts, and without me even realizing, they became …

SECOND THOUGHTS! Judi, I think about you every second of every minute of every hour of every day! Tell me, my love: is there any hope for me? I truly love you that much. You are beautiful!

Honey, I've said this before that I believe that God has put us together and that itself makes our love that much more of a special blessing to me. Judi, you are wonderful. I just know that our threefold cord will not be broken. I do thank God for you and our love for each other!

Well, almost Mrs. Piscitello, I will keep on having second thoughts about you. X O … I miss you. I love you. See you Thursday.

Yours forever,
Charlie

Here's my eventual "reply" in a birthday card to Charlie, many years after we were married:

To Charlie, the Most Wondermous Crepen in the Whole Wide, Wide, Wide World,

It is certainly no coincidence that your birthday follows closely on the heels of Thanksgiving. There is truly nothing in this world for which I am more thankful than the blessing of having you in my life.

When I first met you, I knew there was something very special about you, but as I have grown to love you more and more *every day, every hour, every minute, and every second, I have never had a second thought about whether or not we were meant to spend the rest of our lives together.* I can only thank God that He has put us together for something more wonderful than anything I ever could have imagined.

God has blessed you with so many wonderful talents and skills, such compassion and insight, such tenderness and great strength. You have always been generous in sharing all that you have with me and with our family and friends here today. May He continue to bless you as you live each day in His service, and may you serve Him for many, MANY years to come! Happy birthday, Charlie!

Indeed it was obvious to everyone from the very beginning that God had brought Charlie and me together, and we began to talk of marriage within a few months of that first fateful picnic. Christ was at the center of our relationship—that third cord of the braid Charlie referred to from Ecclesiastes 4:12 that would bind us together in His love forever (1 John 4:8b; Colossians 3:14).

We had toyed with the idea of getting married on December 20, the same day that my mom and dad and my grandparents on my dad's side had gotten married, but there just wasn't enough time to make the gowns and all the other preparations. So we decided to wait until summer so that we could do everything just right—in God's time (Ecclesiastes 3:11).

In addition to strategically spaced phone calls, visits, letters, and cassette tapes, our courtship was highlighted by the exchange of little gifts. The first gift I gave to Charlie was a wind chime, to help him find his way from Frank and Francine's farmhouse to his trailer. This letter (found in Charlie's drawer many years later) accompanied it:

Dear Charlie,

Your voice is like music to my ears, so when I heard these chimes, I knew they were for you. My prayer for you is that your heart will always be in tune with God's Holy Spirit within you, invisibly but powerfully playing the melody line of your life, just as the wind moves through these chimes. Remember John 3:8.

With love in Christ Jesus,
Judi

Charlie's first gift to me was a necklace and earrings set made with mother-of-pearl and gold butterflies. The next time I came to visit, I wore the set proudly. As we were driving to church, I guided his left hand to my right ear.

"Aw! You're wearing your little flutterbies!" He chuckled at twisting the word around.

Attempting to follow suit and intending to say that they made my heart flutter, I tripped over my tongue and replied, "Yes, and they make my farts butter!"

Realizing what had just come out of my mouth, my jaw dropped, I gasped, and we were both laughing so hard that I had to pull the car to the side of the road to gain my composure! From that moment on, I could no longer feign that I was prim and proper. I was *real*.

Charlie and I took turns visiting one another about every two weeks. Crystal would drive up to Churchville and stay with me for the weekend while he would stay with Hans, a man in the Rochester congregation for whom Crystal's heart was, as Charlie would say, "twitterpated," a term that he had gleaned from watching *Bambi*.

Crystal often spoke of kissing a frog to transform it into her Prince Charming. She had even decorated her apartment with all kinds of frogs and flowers and hoped that Hans would one day become her very own Prince Charming.

Referring to Crystal's fanciful frog fetish, one of Charlie's tapes included a song by his favorite artist, Chet Atkins. It was a whimsical version of Ray Stevens's "Frog Kissin'." The song is featured on You Tube and well worth listening: http://www.youtube.com/watch?v=8HQoJo_4_-A.

Whenever Charlie stayed with Hans, he would laugh that Hans always insisted on turning the lights in the bathroom on for him, even though he had no need of them. Hans explained that it just made him feel better that Charlie wasn't groping around in the dark!

Whenever I visited Charlie while we were dating, I would stay with Frank and Francine in their farmhouse so that Charlie and I could be close—but not too close! We asked Francine to check in on us—regularly and unannounced—whenever I visited Charlie's trailer, especially after we became engaged. We were never alone for very long. And that was a God thing.

Although Charlie and I had picked out our rings, he hadn't yet formally popped the question. He was waiting for just the right time to make it memorable. First, he wanted to talk with my father.

When I first told Dad about Charlie, the two hadn't met, so Dad was leery, suggesting that I "forget about the blind guy." Fortunately, I was able to convince him to at least give Charlie a chance by getting to know him.

When we finally found the time to take a weekend to visit Mom and Dad, it was only a matter of minutes before Charlie had them both eating out of the palm of his hand—just as he had charmed the Saratoga concert audience that day I had first laid eyes on him. And just as he had captured my heart, he quickly won theirs as well.

Charlie later wrote to tell me that he'd had a nice talk with my dad on the telephone. He was so happy that the day I would become his bride my dad would become his dad, too.

Once again, Crystal's cupid-like conniving played a part in our engagement. "I hope you like green!" she would tease, over and over again, giggling like a school girl each time I scrunched up my face in puzzlement or begged on the phone for her to tell me what in the world she was talking about.

Springtime had finally come to the farm and it was my turn to visit Charlie. We took a long walk along the creek and returned to Charlie's trailer to wash up for dinner at the farmhouse. Francine had invited a group of our friends from church, including Crystal.

Once back in his living room, Charlie sat me down in a chair that had long ago belonged to his mother. I began to see a twinkle in his eyes as he told me to close mine. As I did, he quietly got down on one knee, slipped the engagement ring onto my finger, and formally yet sweetly asked for my hand in marriage.

One would think that at such a tender moment as this, a woman's response would be to answer yes or no or squeal with delight, but Crystal's teasing had somehow sidetracked my brain.

"It's not green!" I said, looking down at the ring.

"I should hope not!" replied Charlie, bewildered at such an unorthodox response to his marriage proposal.

"But Crystal said it was green!" I tried to explain my puzzled reaction.

Finally catching on, Charlie chuckled. He went across the room to obtain a small, smooth, wooden box and handed it to me. It had a hand-carved tulip on the top and was hinged in the back.

"Open it!" he said, grinning widely.

As I opened the box, I saw that there was a circular well drilled out that was lined with green felt. Charlie had used the wood from an old walnut piano to create the box to hold our wedding rings until we could place them on each other's fingers. He had asked Crystal weeks before whether she thought I would prefer red or green piano felt to line the box. She had hoped that I would like **green**!

Little did I know until then that the gathering of friends for dinner was actually our engagement dinner! The photo on the first page of this chapter was taken in Frank and Francine's living room during the party.

But our most memorable photo of that evening was taken with Charlie and me standing atop a pile of huge boulders that Frank had moved with a bulldozer that very day to decorate the edge of Francine's flower garden. Our soon-to-be marriage began with us standing on a rock—for our marriage was founded upon Jesus Christ, the Rock of our salvation!

The Lord is my rock, my fortress and my deliverer;
my God is my rock, in whom I take refuge, my shield
and the horn of my salvation, my stronghold.
—Psalm 18:2 (NIV)

Our Love

Our love will take a lifetime to grow to its fullest potential.
Our love will be a lifetime of giving and receiving,
Of laughter and tears.
Our love will last a lifetime and beyond.
Our love promises long-term gain,
In spite of, and sometimes because of, short-term pain,
But the cost cannot be compared with the reward!
Our love demonstrates our faith in God and in one another,
By our willingness to work, to suffer, to endure,
And to rejoice in the blessings of one another!
Our love demonstrates a dedication to reaching beyond ourselves
Because we value giving more than receiving,
And yet a great part of our love is based upon our thankfulness
for all that we have received.
Our love must listen carefully and actively, first to understand
and then to confirm our understanding,
Seeking to hear both what is said and what is felt in the Spirit.
Our love desires long-term happiness and security more than
short-term comfort and convenience.
Sometimes our love will hurt but, like birth pangs, will ultimately
bring joy.
Our love must be careful to say no when necessary,
With empathy and compassion, to be firm and yet tender.
Our love will never fail to provide a word, a touch, and a prayer
To encourage one another to endure together.
Our love is a choice we have made to put others above self,
To dedicate ourselves to the lasting happiness of others,
And to their growth and fulfillment, unconditionally.

Though humans may fail for lack of wisdom or abundance of weakness, our love forgives,
Having faith in the good intentions behind them.
Our love holds no expectations of perfection or reward,
Realizes that there will be disagreements and discomforts, separations and frustrations. Our love will endure all.
Our love is the first to encourage, the last to condemn.
Our love is a commitment to the eternal growth and fulfillment
Of all that God has blessed us with, in each other.

—Judi to Charlie, May 19, 1992

Chapter 5

Wind Chimes to Wedding Bells

But seek first the kingdom of God and His righteousness
and all these things will be added to you.
—Matthew 6:33 (NKJV)

The next few months were a flurry of frozen meatballs and aflutter with flowers and frills! Both my church family in

Rochester and his church family in Binghamton/Endicott joined together to help join us as one in the wedding of our dreams! Individuals were enlisted from both congregations according to their talents in providing the flowers, cake, decorations, music, food, photos, video, etc. In addition to choosing all of the music for the ceremony and reception, Charlie's job was to make batches and batches of meatballs and freeze them for the big day!

I made my own gown of satin, lace, and hand-sewn pearls. Francine, my matron of honor, made her gown in a teal floral and Crystal's (my maid of honor) in a matching cranberry floral. Karen's mother made her bridesmaid dress and Barb Simpson made Sarah's junior bridesmaid dress, both in the teal floral.

We all got together and attempted to make our own starched crocheted hats, but the brims either were too stiff or too limp so we decided to make crocheted fans instead as bases for the bridesmaids' bouquets. We also made fans out of flowered wallpaper as wedding favors—very affordable and practical for a July 12 wedding with standing room only!

In place of the crocheted hats that "flopped" (pun intended), we made headpieces of tulle. When the baby's breath and alstroemeria were added to mine on our wedding day, it looked like a crown; I felt like a Scandinavian princess! Even the food was garnished with edible flowers—all from the gardens of our brothers and sisters in Christ. Flowers and paper scrollwork decorated the columns in the downstairs fellowship hall, and the wedding guests came from all over the country to celebrate what God would join together!

What I didn't know until it happened was that my father had asked to be able to speak in response to the minister's question "Who gives this bride to be married?"

"Well, it's often said that the father of the bride gives her away. As father of the bride, I speak for myself; my wife (her mother), her sister, her brother, her niece, and nephew are here. We don't want to give her away, but we will share her with Charlie. So Charlie, I present to you Judi, in love, for marriage. Welcome to our lives, our family, and our hearts."

After the reception, we followed Charlie's friends Tom and Donna Sinclair to our honeymoon get-away in the Pocono's. It was the retirement home of a dear brother in Christ, Uncle Ray, who had built it piece by piece over a period of years along the edge of a winding stream with the deck facing a beautiful waterfall. Uncle Ray loved Charlie but was unable to attend the wedding, and our honeymoon in his home was his wedding gift to us.

Since Tom and Donna knew the way and we didn't, and since it was on their way home to Reading, Pennsylvania, following them seemed the logical thing to do. Charlie had packed a romantic picnic repast of wine, cheese, crackers, pepperoni, and grapes, so when we arrived, we invited them in for something to eat before they continued on their journey home. It had been years since Charlie had seen them, so they had a lot of catching up to do. We talked and laughed for what seemed like hours to Charlie, who couldn't believe he had asked another couple to join us on our wedding night!

Since we hadn't eaten much at the wedding, being barraged by guests we hadn't seen for years, and since Tom and Donna had shared our little picnic meal, all we had was a few grapes left, which Charlie peeled and fed to me in a romantic gesture before asking if he could take me out to dinner.

We went to a little restaurant nearby, and neither of us remembered much about the meal except that when they brought the dinner rolls, the basket contained little cups of Promise margarine. Innocently enough, I asked Charlie if he would like a roll with Promise. Without missing a beat, he quickly replied, "Isn't that what honeymoons are all about?" And then he flashed the brightest, widest, most twinkling grin I had ever seen!

Before we knew it, we were back on the farm and loading up our little Honda Civic (Charlie called it a pregnant roller skate) with Charlie's belongings in order to move him into our little one-bedroom apartment in Churchville. We lived there for a year (sleeping cozily the first two weeks in a single bed until we could purchase a queen-size bed). And then we purchased a home in Batavia, where my office was located—of all places—at the New York State School for the Blind (with workspace in Hamilton Hall, where he had spent those early tough and tender years) and where Charlie would attend Genesee Community College.

Our first two years together were full of momentous events, including getting married, moving first to Churchville and later back to Batavia after enrolling in college, miscarrying our first baby and losing my father to cancer, then losing another baby and later losing my mother (also to cancer) on his birthday the following year. Yet our faith in God and our love for one another was strong and growing stronger in spite of (and possibly even because of) the heartaches.

January 11, 1994

To My Beautiful Judi,

Here we are eighteen months into our marriage and it still seems like just yesterday that we had the ceremony. Yet going back another year to when we met also doesn't seem that long ago. I remember standing there on the grass at that picnic in Corning, watching you drive away with my heart almost breaking, and thinking how much I really wanted you to stay. How very much God has blessed me since then!

Judi, I can't even begin to imagine life without you now. I started out wanting you in my life, but God showed me in a short period of time how much I really needed you. That hasn't and will never change. I am you and you are me. We are one flesh. I need you in my life for the rest of eternity. We are one in spirit with Jesus Christ, and part of His body for eternity.

I love you, Judi. I can't find the words that can tell you adequately how much I do appreciate you as a person first, and then for all that you do to help me. You are a warm and loving and gentle and kind person, and those are the qualities in you that make you radiant and beautiful. I love your smile and your kisses and your little dance you do when you're excited. These, along with all the other nice qualities in you, are what I don't ever want to suppress in you.

I love being your husband, my love. With God supplying the power through His Holy Spirit to keep our marriage together and healthy, I will try not to ever take unlawful or unrighteous advantage of you or my position that God has placed me in with you. I love you forever and ever, Judith Ann Piscitello.

I am yours forever and ever,
—Charlie

I never realized, until I was rummaging through piles of love letters after Charlie died, how many things I'd written either to Charlie or about him. I will share a little poem I had forgotten I'd written:

My Crepen
By Judi Piscitello to her Wondermous Crepen

My Charlie is my crepen, as anyone can see.
You'll always see me smiling, whenever he's with me.

He is the only crepen that ever lived and breathed.
There are no others like him, so don't you be deceived.

My crepen is God's servant, and a shepherd of God's sheep.
His lambs are precious to him; in Christ's love does he keep.

My crepen follows Jesus as best he can, and so,
Because the Lord's his Shepherd, we will know the way to go,

My crepen's music thrills me whenever I hear him play.
It makes me want to praise and sing to Jesus every day!

My crepen always makes me laugh as only he can do.
He makes my life a joy to live; he's precious through and through!

My crepen is a gadget man, a handyman as well.
He'll fix it if it's fixable, the break you'll barely tell.

My crepen's happy most of all when he can mend some hearts
And bring each one to Jesus, dodging Satan's fiery darts.

My crepen's aim within his life is to glorify His King.
That's why I love my crepen, and that's why he makes me sing!

Charlie was very busy that year, completing his associate's degree at GCC, recognized as student of the month and later graduating Phi Theta Kappa and singing the national anthem at his graduation. Thankfully, my mother was able to attend the ceremony and celebrate with us, wearing the same mint-green dress she had worn to our wedding, but this time accessorized with a chemotherapy pack. She was so very brave through it all, and so very proud of her "oldest son!"

Just a few months later, she went into hospice care in her apartment, where my brothers, sisters, and I took turns caring for her. I had spent the night of December 3 with her. The colon cancer had spread to her liver, and the morphine kept her sedated, for the most part. When she woke occasionally during the night moaning weakly, I would hold her close and tell her that I was with her and that I loved her, and she would calm and drift back into oblivion.

The next day was Charlie's birthday, so I felt obligated to return to him, but when I arrived home, Charlie had received "the call" from my brother that Mom had gone to be with the

Lord. Charlie held me as I wept. Unable to celebrate his birthday, he reminded me that Mom was experiencing her own type of birthday in the spirit with Jesus.

Charlie was also very busy remodeling our home, paneling the dining room and stairway and completely remodeling our powder room. He installed a new sink, medicine cabinet, and lighting but needed me to tie a knot in one of the wires to tell which was white and which was black! It made our neighbors very nervous to hear his circular saw running at night in the garage with no lights on, but Charlie and I just laughed. Who needs lights when you have two prosthetic eyes?

If Charlie was busy, I was busier. So much to do, and so little time! I was always rushing around like a white tornado, trying to accomplish just one more thing before going to bed. But Charlie would just smile, pick up his guitar, and begin playing a few bars of the song he had written when we were dating to accompany my reading of Wilfred Arlan Peterson's poem "Slow Me Down, Lord."

Charlie was always buying things, making things, or doing things to show me his love. I am still amazed that he would even think of installing motion-sensor nightlights for me so that I could easily travel around the house at night without having to find a light switch. He would sometimes enlist the services of Jerry, the master carpenter next door, to help him design an intricate gift for me. Two of my favorite gifts were Mrs. Beasley, a Vermont Teddy Bear dressed as an orientation and mobility instructor, complete with a long white cane, and Zeke, a big, white teddy bear, dressed up in overalls, a red bandana, and a cowboy hat.

Together Charlie and Jerry made a beautiful little oak chair for Zeke to sit on. Then they made a guitar-shaped clock for him to hold, with a gold plate engraved, "To Judi with love from Charlie 7/12/92 until forever."

Charlie's favorite place was the garage—his wood shop for "rippin' and snortin'," as he called it—where he spent many happy hours making some new thing or tinkering to fix something old. Nothing went to waste. He always seemed to find some useful purpose for dowels and scraps of wood.

Watching Charlie hammer a nail was nerve-wracking for me. Through the years, he had developed a precise rhythm in letting go of the nail just long enough as the hammer slammed down on it! Charlie never had a fear of a table saw, a drill press, a hammer, or climbing a ladder.

Living in Batavia, we often had ice build up in our gutters and downspouts. One particular year, Charlie traced the source of a leak on our back porch to an ice-clogged downspout on our roof, just outside of our bedroom window. As he headed out the window with a hammer and a rock pick, I pulled him back in by the feet and insisted that he at least let me attach a chain to his belt on one end and to the radiator on the other so that if he slipped he wouldn't slide off the roof onto the driveway below!

Charlie designed and created an extra large wooden mailbox— complete with flag—to hold the extra-large braille packages we often received from the Library for the Blind, braille bills from utility companies, or braille bank statements—not to mention the boxes of therapeutic magnets and bottles of herbs, essential oils, and nutritional supplements he was always ordering! He made lots of shelves over the basement stairs, hidden shelves at the end of the stairway railing, and boxes of all sizes, including window boxes that he hung from the front porch.

Many of the boxes he covered with leftover knotty pine paneling, which he had used to remodel our dining room, living room, powder room, hallways, and stairways. His biggest project was my six-foot-tall knotty-pine "avalanche" cabinet (complete with routed scrollwork), an attempt to somehow contain my overabundance of Tupperware. Stacked high and overflowing, we'd prepare for the avalanche when the door opened!

My sawdust sweetie made shelves for the computer room and used our old kitchen table to make a computer desk, complete with sliding pullout shelves for the keyboard and mouse. He also made sturdy benches for my mother's Duncan Phyfe mahogany table where we had dined for many a large get-together with family, friends, church members, and/or neighbors. When we finally decided to buy a new dining room set, Mom's table and cabinet and Charlie's custom-made benches went to our niece in Carolina so they would stay in the family.

Somewhere, Charlie had found a tremendously oversized guitar pick that was about the size of my fist. He simply labeled it with a plastic braille label, "I picked you!" It's another of my favorite gifts.

Charlie really enjoyed making door chimes as gifts. They were custom-made wooden boxes with a sound hole, across which were stretched metal strings tightened with old harpsichord tuning pegs. Wooden balls suspended from thin dowels would bounce on the metal strings when the door opened to create a beautiful chord. I dearly loved those door chimes, but he gave them all away.

After I retired from my job with the New York State Education Department in 2010, Charlie and I worked together in his "wood shop" (our garage), making quilt racks that we had planned to continue to make and sell at quilt shows and online. He just loved woodworking! Thankfully, we had enough completed for me to give one to each of our daughters-in-law after he passed.

After receiving his associate's degree, Charlie worked as public relations coordinator and counselor at the Genesee Region Independent Living Center, where he had previously worked as an intern. In addition to coordinating annual hot dog stand fundraisers for the center, he gave a "one-man-show" concert at Genesee Community College to raise the funds for the center to purchase a wheelchair-equipped van. The van was needed to transport people with disabilities to various doctor visits and other appointments. Even after the event, the funds kept rolling in from the sale of videos of the concert, to continue operation of the van. Our small Bible study group also supported the center, providing a food pantry to meet the needs of individuals with disabilities and their families.

For many years, Charlie volunteered answering phones for our local crisis hotline, the Regional Action Phone. His tender heart and perceptive ear were much appreciated by the many people who just needed to talk with someone who really cared.

One elderly woman was so lonely she just called to ask the time, knowing that Charlie would continue to engage her in conversation until another caller needed his assistance. Each night he volunteered, he would ask me to pray with him that he could listen with Jesus's heart and speak with Jesus's wisdom to whoever called the hotline.

Charlie and I were also members of the Batavia Lions Club. I was the first female member of the club, and the only female member at the time. We were active members for several years, and Charlie was occasionally asked to play piano for club functions.

As busy as Charlie was throughout his college years, his heart was first and foremost in his worship of and service to the Lord. He and I would often lead worship together in the Rochester congregation, and he was occasionally asked to give sermons there, as well as to lead our ongoing Bible study group during the week in our home.

Charlie's guide dog, Cory, an Australian shepherd, was always included in these gatherings, taking part by offering his trademark amen bark at the end of the final prayer. Because we would travel to church conferences in various locations across the country at least three times a year, Cory became known within our worldwide denomination as "The Amen Dog."

Since our fall conferences would last an entire week, we attended many sermons, and at the end of each sermon, Cory would offer his characteristic amen. This started to annoy Charlie, who felt that the focus of a worship service should be on the Lord and not the dog. So he decided to be proactive at the end of the next sermon by holding his hands over the dog's mouth to prevent him from taking the attention away from Jesus. Later that day, we learned that the pastor who had given the sermon was "concerned"—wondering why the dog hadn't liked his sermon!

Cory was a hardworking guide, and he was always a big attention-grabber for children and other dog lovers of all ages.

When our congregation held a hot dog stand as a fundraiser every year, Cory was our honorary hot dog boss (although he preferred burgers). And like any good servant leader, he was never too proud to clean up whatever dropped around the stand!

Here he is relaxing on the patio with a burger after a long "dog day" at the hot dog stand! I think he looks quite handsome in his shades, don't you?

I have often wondered at the amazing way in which God brought Charlie and me together at just the right time in our lives. As much as we are told that His timing is perfect, there is nothing sweeter than seeing Him working out His perfect plan "up close and personal."

I once heard somewhere that if women would just run after the Lord like we run after men, Jesus would gladly send us a man we wouldn't have to run after! All my life, I had been searching for the perfect husband, but I hadn't sought out The

Perfect Matchmaker until I had learned to trust and obey Him. Only my Creator knew just the right one for His plan, and only when I had totally surrendered to His plan would He make that connection happen.

Likewise, Charlie had been searching for fame and fortune in the music business, but he eventually learned that there were greater treasures in heaven. Like Moses, who had rubbed elbows with rich and powerful kings and princes in Egypt (a land of sinful idol worship), God took Charlie away from an idolatrous lifestyle and allowed him to dwell humbly in the wilderness (in a rundown, old trailer on an organic dairy farm in central New York State) before rewarding his faithfulness with a calling to ministry.

God's love is a different kind of love. He doesn't love what is of value; instead, He creates value in what He loves. When others saw a shepherd boy, God saw a king in David. When others saw a poor, blind piano tuner living in a broken-down trailer on a friend's dairy farm, God saw Charlie's passion for Christ and His gospel and a tenderness for God's people that his blind eyes enhanced by forcing him to focus his ears on their hearts without the distraction of outward appearances.

Our Faithful Shepherd was also present in the small things, taking my childhood fascination with Helen Keller and Anne Sullivan and my desire to become a teacher and slowly narrowing my field of vision (pun intended) until I settled into a career teaching children who were blind or visually impaired. He knew that this background would help me to be instrumental in providing my husband with the latest assistive technology to enable him to complete college and fulfill His plan for Charlie to serve His children in Batavia as their faithful shepherd.

Chapter 6

"The Changes"

But grow in the grace and knowledge of our Lord and Savior
Jesus Christ. To Him be the glory both now and forever. Amen.
—2 Peter 3:18 (NKJV)

Throughout the early years of our marriage, our denomination was undergoing gradual but radical change from cult status into mainstream Christian doctrine. When these changes began to be discussed, there was obviously a great deal of confusion and a wide variety of emotions among members. Some even left the denomination to join splinter groups, and others were too overwhelmed to make any decision until they learned where this new road was taking them.

At one point in our denomination's transformation journey, our pastor was encouraging us to prayerfully ask God to reveal His truth about the direction He wanted us to go. The pastor confided that he was just as confused as anyone but that he had learned in the Navy that when the waters are rough, the safest place to be is in the ship. He encouraged us to wait out the storm together with him, trusting that God would eventually calm the raging sea and save His people.

In less than a year, in spite of losing a large portion of the thousands of members in our denomination, the Worldwide Church of God transitioned "From the Fringe to the Fold," as stated by Ruth Tucker in her article with that title in the July 15, 1996 edition of *Christianity Today*. Following those unprecedented doctrinal changes, our denomination also made sweeping changes in our approach to preaching the gospel, instituting small cell groups such as ours and ordaining many "bivocational pastors," including Charlie.

Pastoral candidates and their wives were sent in waves to the denominational headquarters in Pasadena for pastoral training. Our training was in the summer of 1997, and we held our first worship service in our home on January 31, 1998. Just as Charlie had prayed before we were married, we had built our house (our marriage) seeking godly wisdom. And in following God's wisdom, our home had eventually become our Father's house—a house of prayer.

Our little congregation quickly became a close-knit family under the loving leadership and guidance of its shepherd leader.

Pastor Charlie encouraged each member to utilize the gifts that God had given in service within the family, church, and community. Each member was likewise encouraged to take part in worship services, setting up and taking down the chairs, podium, sound equipment, and other furnishings as needed, taking turns acting as a worship leader, Scripture reader, prayer intercessor, sound engineer, etc., in addition to other tasks within the congregation. As Jesus had taught in Matthew 25:40, service to others was encouraged by Pastor Charlie as if it were service to Christ Himself.

Because he was the only one in our little congregation with a gift of instrumental music, Pastor Charlie would use an electronic piano at worship services, playing all of the music as well as giving the sermon. In the later years, however, in order to avoid the appearance of a one-man show and to be able to focus more closely on his sermon, he would prerecord the music on his Clavinova electronic piano at home.

Pastor Charlie encouraged the worship leader to choose songs that complemented the sermon message for the week and would then invite them to come to our home some time prior to the service. Using his Clavinova, he would play each song, adding layers of instrumentation to his taste, then record each song in the order needed for the worship service. This would include congregational hymns and special music as well as offertory and communion music, all recorded on cassette tape during the early years and later to CD.

Peggy, one of the older women in our little church family, was unable to attend services, due to the traveling distance and her failing health. But that didn't keep her from being an active member of our congregation! Pastor Charlie made certain that we visited her regularly and that she was able to take part in our worship services by recording the Scripture reading that would support the sermon.

Peg's recording would then be played at the appropriate time during the service, which was tape-recorded in the early years and later videotaped and mailed to her, so that she would always feel that she played an integral part in the worship service each week. Peg also crocheted mittens and slippers for us and for people in local nursing homes and for the children at the school for the blind.

In addition, Peg crocheted baby items for All Babies Cherished, the local pregnancy assistance center at which Pastor Charlie and I occasionally counseled new parents. Just before she passed away, she crocheted a little sparkling-white model of a church, telling us that she was praying that one day we would have our own church building.

Pastor Charlie also led our congregation in providing worship services once a month at the two local nursing homes. The people really seemed to enjoy Pastor Charlie's lively music and sermons!

Early in the history of our little flock, as a service to people with disabilities in our denomination, our congregation purchased a high-speed multi-cassette recorder. We did this in order to provide tape-recorded readings of the denomination's publications to those all over the United States and Canada who were unable to read print due to blindness or other disability. The denomination provided address labels for those who requested cassette copies of church publications, along with cassette mailers designed to be sent Free Matter for the Blind or Physically Handicapped through the United States Postal Service.

For many years, the denomination had provided this service for Charlie, and he took great pleasure in giving back by enabling others to access church publications as well. Pastor Charlie also offered disability awareness workshops to area churches in order to encourage full access to all church activities. "After all," he would occasionally say, "we all suffer from the disability of sin."

On July 17, 1999, Charlie's ordination was recognized in the receipt of his certificate of ordination to the ministry of Jesus Christ. On October 17, 2001, the Batavia Christian Fellowship (BCF) received its charter as Local Congregation #1093 of the Worldwide Church of God.

Each year we would have a hot dog stand fundraiser, as Pastor Charlie had done with the Center for Independent Living, and each year we would have a church family picnic, inviting other churches in the community to join us. BCF became an active part of the Batavia church community and was one of many involved in promoting and participating in what became known as "Unity Services" held monthly at various churches.

Unity in the Body of Christ was a very high priority for Pastor Charlie, as he believed it is to Jesus, as evidenced in His prayer in John 17. He encouraged our congregation to fellowship in one another's homes as well as at church activities, telling us that our best friends should be our brothers and sisters in the Lord. On numerous occasions, we would join with another local congregation for combined worship services, as we worked to build unity in our community through the churches.

Because at the time Pastor Charlie was the president and I was the secretary of the Genesee Council of Churches, which later became the Genesee County Churches United and is now Genesee County Outreach Ministry, we encouraged brothers and sisters in Christ all over Genesee County to work together to meet the spiritual needs of the community, sponsoring and coordinating the County Jail Ministry as well as the Food Pantry Ministry, administered by the local Salvation Army. Along with the Gideons, local pastors and lay teachers serve in the jail to provide worship services, Bible studies, and spiritual guidance to inmates and their families, with volunteers from each church being assigned for an entire month in order to provide continuity.

Bibles and Daily Bread devotionals are provided at the jail, along with other supplemental Christian literature. At Christmas time the jail ministry provides Christmas boxes to the inmates containing items such as candy, soap, toothpaste, a pair of socks, and writing materials to encourage inmates to keep in touch with loved ones.

When Pastor Charlie brought Cory into the jail, he was amazed at how well behaved the inmates were. He later learned that some of the inmates had thought Cory was a drug dog!

Pastor Charlie Piscitello, Senior Pastor, Batavia
Christian Fellowship, Batavia, New York.

Through my affiliation with the Salvation Army as an advisory board member and Women's Auxiliary member, we became acquainted with the majors at the Salvation Army. Charlie quickly became good friends with Major Leslie Jordan, and when our congregation outgrew our home, we were invited to worship on Saturdays at their worship enter, as their worship services were on Sundays and the building was not in use on Saturdays. This was in the early years, when our denomination was still in transition from our Saturday Sabbath worship to Sunday worship.

We welcomed the opportunity to worship in a building designed for worship that also had facilities for meals, Bible classes, and meetings. Because Batavia was a central location for our district, our denomination was able to hold many of its district leadership meetings, worship leader training, and marriage seminars at the Salvation Army building where we held our worship services.

Just as it had happened throughout Charlie's life, whenever he would begin to get close to a man who was a father figure or mentor to him, something would happen that would remove that man from Charlie's life. Much to Charlie's dismay, Major Jordan was transferred.

It was through Major Boynton, who had replaced Major Jordan, that we became aware of the need for volunteers on the local Salvation Army Disaster Team. Several members of our congregation joined with Pastor Charlie and me in serving meals to local fire fighters while they worked to fight a particularly challenging fire affiliated with a train derailment.

Pastor Charlie quickly became friends with Major Boynton as well, and our little congregations would occasionally join together for worship services. When their congregation was in need of Sunday school teachers, Pastor Charlie became the teacher for the men while I had the sweet pleasure of teaching the preschoolers. Major Boynton later became the president of Genesee County Churches United, as the Salvation Army administered our local food pantry ministry.

During the time that Batavia Christian Fellowship met at the Salvation Army, I found it necessary to have surgery on my right foot. Unable to put weight on my foot, this proved to be quite a challenge with regard to driving and grocery shopping. I learned that I could put my big, booted right foot on Charlie's side of the car in order to use my left foot for the gas and brake. However, verbally directing Charlie to push my wheelchair with a grocery cart strapped in front (while Cory tagged along beside) proved to be quite a dog and pony show!

Shortly after another surgery, this time on my leg, in the middle of a worship service, one of our members suddenly slumped over in his seat. A dear, sweet, older gentleman, one of our deacons, had varicose veins. While seated in the pew next to his fiancée, one of his veins had burst, unbeknownst to anyone, and he passed out from loss of blood.

The Holy Spirit took over as Pastor Charlie directed me to call 911 and then asked the ladies to pray. The Prince of Peace gave us all a sense of calmness that He was in control, and He guided us swiftly into action. Thankfully, I was wearing an Ace bandage on my leg that I was able to wrap tightly around our dear brother's elevated leg, to at least slow any further bleeding.

Pastor Charlie continued to pray as the ambulance arrived to take this dear man to the hospital, where they at first could not find a pulse. But God is faithful, and He answered our prayers.

Just a few months later, Pastor Charlie performed the deacon's wedding in our home. Such a joyous occasion for such sweet saints! Major Boynton praised God that the insurance claim for the bloodstains had paid for a long overdue new carpet for the Salvation Army's sanctuary!

While working as Student Support Coordinator for students with disabilities at Genesee Community College, Pastor Charlie worked diligently to bring the gospel to students and faculty alike. He facilitated the Intervarsity Christian Fellowship group and invited international students into our home for a special Thanksgiving celebration each year.

We also invited these students for a summer picnic. Looking back at the photo of that picnic, I am pleasantly surprised to see that several students who had attended that picnic had gotten married! Two of the students had wanted Pastor Charlie to officiate their weddings, but unfortunately his health at that time did not allow him to travel out of state.

A Day in the Life of the Wife of a Man
Who Just Happens to Be Totally Blind
(Or Teaching Them Is One Thing; Living
with Them Is Another!)
By Judi Piscitello, TVI, COMS, 1999

At 6:00 a.m. I awaken to a talking alarm clock obnoxiously proclaiming, "Your attention please! It is now 6 a.m. Please hurry!" A bird clock chirps in the hallway as I go downstairs to let out my husband's guide dog (the "honor" of the first one who happens to get out of bed in the morning). I kick the "dirty rat" dog toy across the living room onto the dog's bed on my way to the kitchen to draw a big glass of water to take my nutritional supplements (with braille labels on the bottles).

At 6:08 I check my weight on our talking scale. The scale has no mercy, proclaiming my weight loudly enough to wake the dead, and then has the nerve to say, "Have a nice day!" After my shower, I lay out a matching shirt, tie, and suit jacket for my husband. (We really don't have the time to sew in braille labels that will just fall off like buttons anyway!) All his socks are black, for the sake of my sanity.

As my husband enters sleepily into the bathroom, I warn him to keep to the right of my vanity chair, which I had pulled out from under the vanity counter. I must always be sure to close all doors, drawers, and cupboards and keep walkways, chairs, and common table surfaces as clear as possible. This is no easy task. A common phrase around our household is "No careening!"

At 6:23 a.m., my personal grooming is interrupted by his requests for me to read printed matter of various types (mail, prescription restrictions, receipts left in his pocket, etc.). Because I'm trying to put on my makeup, he holds the paper out for me to read. "Turn it over. No, now it's upside down. Oh, just give it to me!"

At 6:50 a.m., I drive my husband to Dunkin' Donuts because it's his turn to provide the bagels for coffee break. I guide him inside and caution him to stay close, as many customers are crowding between the counter and the door, and the guide dog is in the car because he'd just make it worse.

We order eighteen bagels, six for his office and a dozen for mine, discussing his office preferences, as he can't see the flavor choices and I don't know his colleagues' preferences. I leave my husband (as collateral) eating breakfast at Dunkin' Donuts while I drive to the supermarket for cash. When we left the house he insisted we had enough money to buy bagels for our offices. But he'd forgotten his wallet, and even all the change in the toll dispenser in the car didn't make it. (Note: this is a man thing, *not* to be blamed on blindness!) At 7:51 a.m., I drop him off and drive to work (with dog hair sticking to the water condensed on the outside of the Coolata cup).

After work, I pick up my husband from his job as Public Relations Coordinator at the Genesee Region Independent Living Center and drive to the ATM to deposit his paycheck. The ATM drive-up window has braille on the keys. Get real! (I have a license plate holder on my car that says, "Caution: Driver reads Braille," but it doesn't keep the tailgaters off my bumper!)

Anyhow, this ATM drive-up has braille on the keys, but using the ATM also requires responding to what is on the screen. Since the screen doesn't talk, should my husband sit in my lap so he can read the braille while I read him the screen?

Maybe I should just teach him to memorize the locations of the buttons and the sequence of operations called for on the screen, take his chances that he's pushed the right buttons, and pray that the machine is working properly. But I really don't think the guy in the pick-up behind me (whose Dobermans are barking at our guide dog) would understand if my husband and I get out of the car to have a lesson on using the ATM!

At 4:48 p.m., we drive to the hardware store and lumber yard to pick up two-by-fours, plywood, and other items needed for my husband to make a sandwich sign for our church fundraiser. We both approach the counter, and I guide him up to the clerk and turn away from him so that the clerk will talk to my husband, not me.

Most people seem to be more comfortable talking to someone who gives them eye contact. But since my husband is very sociable and knowledgeable about woodworking, I just get out of his way in order to make sure he's the one to talk with the clerk. I learned this avoidance tactic because once, a few years ago, I had accompanied my husband to a new place to get his hair cut. When we walked into the salon, the stylist greeted us and my husband asked if she could take a walk-in. She turned to me and asked, "Does he want a haircut?"

My husband answered, "I sure would," to which she responded, "Then bring him over here, get his coat off him, and sit him down in the chair!"

I guided him to the coat rack and he put his coat on a hook. I guided him to the chair where he seated himself, and then I left the salon so that he could do his public awareness thing with her. By the time I came back, his "ears were lowered" and she was actually treating him like a real person!

Anyway, when we go back to pick up the lumber, it's me with the two-by-four hoisted over my shoulder so I can eyeball it to see if it's warped. At 5:13 p.m., we stop at the grocery store to pick up a few items for dinner. Children in various locations around the store exclaim, "Doggie!" as we go by. Some parents just say, "Yes, Doggie," others say, "That's a *special* doggie," and others say, "No, you can't pet the doggie because he's working." Still others just try

119

to get the kid to be quiet by quickly moving away from the doggie.

We often stop to let the children pet the dog, explaining that they can only pet dogs when they've asked the owner's permission. We explain about the harness and the doggie's job to keep the owner safe.

Adults also notice the dog and will usually either compliment us on him or ask his name. When people ask what kind of dog he is, my husband will first respond that he's a guide dog, even though he's fully aware of the fact that what they really want to know is the breed (Australian shepherd). That's his way of saying that people are supposed to ignore the dog when he's working. The dog used to wear a sign to that effect, but nobody ever paid any attention to it.

One woman didn't say one word to my husband and actually fed the dog while my husband was walking with him. I had to run interference so the dog wouldn't walk my husband into a huge display of buy-one-get-one potato chip bags!

The trips to the grocery store were even more fun last fall when I had foot surgery and had to be in a wheelchair for eight weeks. We'd either get a motorized cart I could drive with husband and dog following behind (and sometimes passing because the dog wasn't paying attention) or we'd get a cart that could be attached to the wheelchair with Velcro straps. This was quite a dog and pony show!

One day, the electric cart was out of order and we couldn't get a wheelchair cart that I could propel myself. I tried to direct my husband in pushing the wheelchair cart. "Left a little … Slow down … Right a little … Stop. Stop. Stop!" (as someone innocently walked in front of the cart)! This was so unnerving that we finally had to ask for someone to push my wheelchair cart and get the groceries off the shelves while my husband and I kind of came along for the ride.

To drive home, I'd have to drive with my left foot, throwing the right foot in the surgical boot over the hump to my husband's side of the car. He'd put the wheelchair in the back of the van, and when we got home, he'd wheel me up the ramp he'd built to the front door. Hauling that wheelchair around sure didn't help his back any.

Anyway, at 5:45 p.m., we finally get into the checkout line. My husband and I put the groceries on the belt. Then while I'm trying to write the check, scan my card, and put away the change and receipt, the dog does his usual "Gimme a treat 'cuz I'm cute" routine, jumping up with front paws on the register to startle the clerk while my husband looks around for his favorite candy bar. The dog learned this nifty trick at K-Mart, where one of the clerks keeps treats at her register for whenever we come into the store, whether she's there or not.

Finally we get out to the van and open the hatch to put the groceries inside. Unaware that the woman in the pickup next to us could hear every word, my husband asks me to pull his thumb. Because my chiropractor often does this to me as an adjustment for pain in my wrist, I thought nothing of it and pulled his thumb, at which point he released the gas from the baked beans he'd had at lunch! I don't know who laughed harder—my husband, the lady in the pickup, or me!

At 5:45 p.m., we drive home and cook dinner together, using the microwave I'd adapted with braille and jars and cans of food he'd opened yesterday when I wasn't home that weren't labeled with braille and didn't turn out to be what he wanted. We've learned to be creative in combining miscellaneous items like cans of asparagus and marinated mushrooms with a jar of sun-dried tomatoes to make some pretty interesting pasta dishes!

My husband's adapted slicing knife is the envy of our friends, as it has an adjustable guide to slice onions, tomatoes, cucumbers, bagels, or what-have-you at whatever thickness you desire. My husband gets ice cubes out of the icemaker, but I get to pick up the ones that drop and go sliding across the floor under the table. (He has a bad back.)

After dinner, I reprogram all of our digital clocks, along with the air conditioner and VCR, as last night's thunderstorm made the power go out, and most digital devices are not accessible to people who are blind.

My husband is the pastor and the pianist for our church. At 7:00 p.m., I type and translate into braille the key Scriptures for his sermon, as well as the list of songs for our upcoming worship service, along with the key signature and number of verses. Brailling is done on my husband's talking computer with a special translation program and a braille printer. He also has a talking braille-input laptop. Both computers can be used for e-mail and Internet access, although non-text attachments must be sent to me, as these are not accessible to him.

At 8:45 p.m., I check the rest of my e-mail on my computer. I reformat the e-mail and attachments my husband needs, also removing the ">" and "=20" from these for more understandable reading with speech, and resend to his text-based e-mail account.

At 9:34 p.m., my husband comes in from the garage to ask me to come outside and tell him which side of the plywood is the nicest looking so that he can have that side facing outward for the sandwich sign. While I'm out there, he also asks if I would please locate the last three special screws he'd dropped on the floor that had rolled under his table saw. He'd found the other thirteen screws himself using a magnet on a stick, but between not knowing where they were and his bad back, he just couldn't get the last three. I had to turn the light on in the garage to find them.

The week we moved to Batavia, my husband had been sawing some wood out in the garage late one evening. The neighbors called, quite upset that they heard the saw but the lights weren't on in the garage!

At 11:30 p.m. as I'm getting ready for bed, I hear a blood-curdling yell from my husband on the stairway. The dog had left a bone on the stairs, and my husband had twisted his ankle on it. Then I notice that he's stripped down to his shorts, the draperies are open downstairs, and he's essentially "on TV" for anyone who might be looking through the windows to see him prancing around in his undies, not to mention calling attention to himself by screaming on the stairway! He just doesn't seem to care that people might see him in his skivvies. Is that a guy thing or because he's blind?

My husband insists that the fans and air conditioners be turned off so he can sleep, because he's sick of hearing motors all day. (Before we got the new refrigerator, he'd even unplug the old one while we were eating because it was so loud.) Then he turns on the radio next to his bed and plugs in the earplug so as not to disturb me.

I'm hot, and he's still got noise in his ear. Is this a guy thing, a blind-guy thing, or just my husband's thing?

In the middle of the night, he wakes up and can't get back to sleep. I wake up to the swish-swish of his fingers going across the pages of his braille Bible, thankful that at least he didn't need to turn the light on to read!

Yes, indeed! Teaching them is one thing; living with them is quite another!

What a blessing it was that Charlie caught on so quickly to the assistive technology designed for people who are blind. Charlie quickly endeared himself to many of the TVIs (teachers of the visually impaired) all over New York State, troubleshooting with them over the phone whenever they had problems with a Braille'nSpeak laptop computer or JAWS (Job Access With Speech) talking software.

Because I was on the road so much traveling across the state for my job, Charlie insisted that I always be reachable by phone in case of emergency. When we went from the old bag phone to the cell phone to OnStar, Charlie was much relieved indeed that I could talk hands free while driving. One day while I was refueling the minivan, Charlie called and OnStar automatically connected the call. Because the doors and windows were closed, I could barely hear his voice. I didn't want to stop pumping gas so I yelled, "I'm getting gas and I can't let go!" It wasn't until I heard his unmistakable laughter that I realized what I had said!

At least 50 percent of his waking hours, Charlie was either listening to music, or to a sermon, or a talk show on the radio or playing music on the piano, guitar, or mandolin the congregation gave to him. One Sunday evening as Charlie was serenading me with his guitar, I asked him what he was playing, and he said that it was a song that he'd written a long time ago. It was a love song, and as I listened, I quickly wrote down the words, making him play it a few more times until I was certain I had all the lyrics. He said that the name of the song was "'Til Time Stands Still."

'Til Time Stands Still
By Charlie Piscitello

God willing, I'll have your precious love
Sent to me from up above
To cherish and hold for eternity
And prove how faithful my love can be.
God willing, I'll love you with all my heart
And pray that we will never ever part.
And my love, I'll prove to you
The many things that I can do

To hold your hand in a time warp,
To cheer you up when you're feeling low,
To solve your every problem, dear,
To wipe away your every little tear,

To hold you through your fear
And brush away every little tear.
Yes, my love, God willing, I will
Love you too, 'till time stands still,
'Til time stands still,
'Til time stands still!

Amidst the huge box full of love letters that accumulated over our twenty-one years together, I found a yellowed sheet of tractor-feed printer paper containing this undated letter from Charlie:

Hello my friend, my love, my wife!

I hope that our life together (our marriage) will always be a part of your prayer list. God is our refuge and our strength. Remember Proverbs 24:3-5. If we build our house on anything other than God's wisdom, it will fall apart in a time of trouble because the foundation just won't be there to sustain the trial.

I love you. I love you, Judi Piscitello. Read this again and again until you really understand what I'm saying. It's you and you only that I love. For better or for worse, etc., I love you, Judi. I do pray for you and for us. Remember our threefold cord: with Christ Jesus, all things are possible. With God, nothing is impossible. I love you forever and ever. Amen.

I also found a handful of handmade braille cards from Charlie. The front of one of these cards says, "Thinking of You!" Under this, there is a big open space in the center of the card. "I'm sending you a hug and a kiss to let you know it's you I miss."

Inside the card, which is an eight-and-a-half-inch by eleven-inch sheet of braille paper, folded in half and then in half again, Charlie drew a big circle for the hug and an X for the kiss. Inside on the right hand side, the card reads,

Dear Judi,

The picture on the front of this card is you and I standing on the rock in the middle of the creek on that Sabbath morning on the farm. I love you. I am your Charlie.

One night, after we had been married for quite some time, when I was getting ready to go to bed, I found a check on my pillow. Charlie, in his unmistakable handwriting, had pledged to pay one million kisses, for deposit into our lifetime account and redeemable upon request forever and ever.

Many times when Charlie wrote a letter, he would fold it into thirds and write part of a sentence on the outside section and the rest underneath when you lift up that third. On one such letter, on the top of the folded letter as it came out of the envelope, Charlie wrote, "Judi, you are my ..." And on the other third underneath, he wrote, "Sunshine!" The letter went on to thank me for my letter with the prose about love (See page 89), as he had needed some encouragement that particular day and God sent my letter to put the smile back on his face.

Another message from Charlie, sent by mail when we were dating, was a handwritten letter on raised-line writing paper, containing strips of lines of a braille love letter that he had cut up. The handwritten letter says,

Hi, Honey.

Please forgive me. I got carried away with trimming the paper down and now just look at it! I hope you can put it together again! I love you. I miss you.

—Your Charlie.

Thankfully, I was able to assemble the lines in the proper order to form a beautiful love poem that will remain between my Wondermous Crepen and me.

Years before we met, Charlie had traveled with Karen and Richard Carpenter, and one of his tapes to me included their song "Close to You," along with one of his precious quartered braille paper cards. On the front, he brailled, "I am not whole without you in my life." He left a space for his imaginary picture in the middle, and at the bottom, he brailled, "I do so long to be *Close to You.*"

Inside, he brailled,

> The picture on the front is Mr. Kubik [the pastor that officiated our wedding], you, and me, in his house, sitting and talking about our future. Your face is glowing. I know that because he said so, also because I really can see it for myself. I thank God for you, Judi. I love you.

Chapter 7

Faith, Not Sight

*Therefore we do not lose heart. Though outwardly we are
wasting away, yet inwardly we are being renewed day by
day. For our light and momentary troubles are achieving
for us an eternal glory that far outweighs them all. So we
fix our eyes not on what is seen, but on what is unseen, since
what is seen is temporary, but what is unseen is eternal.*
—2 Corinthians 4:16–18 (NIV)

Eventually, after our denominational transition had run its
full course, we desired to begin having our worship services

on Sundays instead of Saturdays. This meant that we could no longer remain at the Salvation Army, so we moved our little church family to the local YWCA building.

It was at the YWCA that we met Pastor Dave and Eileen Appleton and their church family known as the Heart of Christ Fellowship. We were renting the room with the kitchen facilities in the back for our worship services, and they rented the room across the hall that we used Wednesday evenings for our Bible studies. Pastor Dave volunteered at the Open Door Mission in Rochester and earned his living as a carpenter—a carpenter on a mission, just like Jesus!

After receiving training in Christian counseling through the American Association of Christian Counselors in basic counseling skills as well as in marriage counseling, Charlie and I were asked to counsel couples at All Babies Cherished, the local pregnancy assistance center. These "listening to people's hearts" skills were also put to use at the college and in our congregation as well as with his crisis hot-line work and Care-A-Van Ministries in the prayer ministry.

In 2005, having gradually gained almost one hundred pounds throughout our marriage, I began to radically change my eating habits and began a more vigorous exercise program to lose weight. Yet in spite of my diligent efforts over many months, the weight remained, and Charlie suggested that something must be wrong with my thyroid gland. I decided to consult an endocrinologist, and God directed me to just the right doctor, who identified my weight gain as the result of Cushing's disease.

Cushing's is a rare condition (one in a million) in which a tumor secretes adrenocorticotropic hormone (ACTH), in turn causing the adrenal gland to secrete cortisol, the stress hormone.

Cortisol causes the body to build body fat in the torso, including a "buffalo hump" of extra fat across the shoulder blades and extra weight in the face and chin, known as "moon face," along with other unpleasant symptoms, such as stretch marks, excess facial hair, and skin infections. The tumors are usually found either in the adrenal or pituitary glands but can sometimes be ectopic— elsewhere in the body—and can be cancerous.

I began to research Cushing's online and learned that it is often very difficult to diagnose and that those who have had the most success in locating and eliminating the tumors are those who seek out hospitals and doctors who specialize in Cushing's and related diseases. Thankfully, my health insurance covered the diagnostic processes and procedures as well as the surgery to remove the tumor. My insurance even paid for my prayer partner, Eileen Appleton, to travel with me to Boston's Massachusetts General Hospital for both the procedure to locate the tumor (inferior petrosal sinus sampling with CRH stimulation) and the surgery to remove it.

In the process of my diagnosis, I learned that I had an even more rare form of Cushing's—the cyclic type that was not a constant secretion but an occasional drip. In my case, it was every four days.

When the doctor told me that they had found the tumor they believed was responsible for the Cushing's in my pituitary gland, I replied, "Praise the Lord!"

Shocked at my response, the doctor questioned, "You're praising the Lord that you have a brain tumor?"

"Yes," I reasoned. "I know I need to get the tumor out in order to cure the Cushing's. If it's in my adrenal gland, they have to cut me open and it's major surgery, right?"

The doctor nodded.

"And if it's anywhere else, it could be one crazy cancerous cell that we might never find, right?"

He nodded again.

"But with a pituitary tumor, they go through the nose and I'm out of the hospital the same day. Is that correct?"

"Well, I guess you've done your homework, haven't you?" he said with a smile.

When Charlie learned that I needed to fly to Boston for brain surgery, he assembled the congregation to pray for me and thanked Eileen for accompanying me. I knew he was afraid for me, but I also knew that his faith was strong and we both knew for a fact that God is good.

On the way to the hospital in the cab, Eileen was talking to the cab driver about Jesus. The driver told Eileen that he was Muslim but that he would occasionally be given Christian tracts, which he would read and then pass on to others. We later chuckled at the thought of a Muslim evangelist for Jesus!

During the previous ten years, I'd undergone two surgeries on my left leg and two minor surgeries on my feet. But, believe it or not, none of those surgeries was as easy as my brain surgery. As it turned out, my surgery was scheduled to begin at 10:00 a.m. At 7:00 that evening, as Eileen and I were eating dinner in a Boston restaurant, I remember saying to the waitress, "I can't believe I had brain surgery this morning!" God, indeed, is very good!

Like most little girls, having children of my own had been my life-long dream. I had never aspired to be rich or famous. All I had ever wanted was to be the best wife and mother I could be, which was why I had pursued a career as a teacher. I wanted to teach my children well. I wanted to provide the very best I could for them. I wanted to enjoy being home with them evenings, weekends, holidays, and summer vacations.

When I had learned I was pregnant early in our marriage, I was ecstatic! But our joy was short-lived, as I quickly miscarried. We tried once again, and once again I miscarried. The pain of losing our babies was multiplied when I had to sign an infant death certificate after having the D&C needed following the miscarriage. I wondered how many women would have multiple abortions if they had to sign an infant death certificate for each one?

As my biological clock ticked away, so did my hope of having children of our own. Yet Charlie would not agree to adoption this late in his life. He had seen too many adoptions go awry, and he was not willing to press his luck at age fifty, especially since he had heart problems, possibly leaving me a widow with a child.

When Charlie had married his first wife, he had adopted her son Donald as his very own. He never allowed anyone to refer to Donny as "adopted" or a "stepson." Charlie said that he had adopted Donny just as God adopts us—as full sons and daughters with all responsibilities, rights, and privileges. Donny felt Charlie's love deeply as a child, and when he became of age, he surprised his father by taking on a first name that sounded better with Piscitello: Dominic. That was also his uncle's name.

When Charlie and I became engaged, his son Dominic wrote him a card that congratulated his father in finding someone to share the rest of his life with. Dominic vowed to honor me, and he has faithfully kept that promise to this day. I am blessed and so very thankful for Dom and his ever-growing family (he is now the proud grandfather of three with another on the way), who have always made me feel loved like family.

In 2003 when my doctor advised a hysterectomy due to fibroid tumors throughout my uterus, my already shattered dream of biological children was finally dashed into an explosion of tears. Charlie held me as I sobbed uncontrollably with grief.

Encouraging me gently by reading from Isaiah 54, "my Boaz" (Ruth 2:20) calmed my broken heart by reminding me that I was the "mother" of our little church family and that I could continue to bring spiritual children of all ages to Father God throughout my lifetime—gleaning a spiritual harvest for His eternal kingdom family (Psalm 126:5–6 NIV). It wasn't until my follow-up visits at Massachusetts General Hospital that I learned that the extremely high levels of cortisol due to the Cushing's disease might have contributed to my miscarriages. By then I had resigned my heart to believe that if children were not in God's plan for me, then He must have something even better in store.

Not long after my brain surgery, Pastor Charlie began to join the Care-A-Van prayer ministry (www.cavministries.org). Care-A-Van Ministries had begun in December 1999, when Paul and Bridget Ohlson, along with their two daughters, decorated their motor home in order to bring Christmas to a number of needy people they knew of in Batavia.

As Paul's family and their growing group of supporters continued to minister to more and more people in several Batavia neighborhoods, they saw their great need for groceries. So in May 2000, they began to park on the corner of Batavia's State Street to pass out free groceries.

By November, they realized they needed a different kind of vehicle in order to adequately address the multiple needs of the people. Therefore, they purchased an old fire-rescue truck.

During the summers, the Care-A-Van rescue truck (painted bright red and adorned with encouraging Scriptures) would be packed up with all the makings of a picnic: hot dogs, hamburgers, rolls, condiments, potato and macaroni salad, baked beans, watermelon, punch, and sometimes ice cream—along with folding tables and chairs enough for a street picnic in a small city neighborhood.

A pickup truck would carry two grills, and a few Christian musicians would bring their musical equipment. A local pastor would volunteer to preach a short sermon, and the neighborhood would be fed both physically and spiritually by Christians from various denominations who saw what God was doing with the ministry and wanted to join in serving.

I would occasionally bring a silly hat or some puppets to entertain the children. Sometimes Pastor Charlie would preach and sometimes he would play his keyboard or guitar, but he would always pray with folks in the neighborhoods we visited.

In 2007, an old city bus was donated to the ministry. The back of the bus was customized to accommodate a mobile food pantry outreach and the front was used weekdays for prayer ministry. Monday through Thursday, the bus parks somewhere in Batavia and a sandwich sign is placed just outside the front door, inviting folks to come inside for free coffee, prayer, and encouragement.

Paul gave Pastor Charlie a guided tactile-auditory tour of the newly renovated bus, letting Charlie explore both the exterior and interior as he described the Scriptures and other features of the bus. He even let Pastor Charlie sit in the driver's seat!

Little did Paul know at the time that one of Charlie's dreams was to get together all of the people who had ever given him a ride in any kind of vehicle throughout his life, put them all in a bus, and give them the ride of their lives. He said he hoped Jesus would let him do that someday, maybe even giving folks a bus ride through the clouds, just for fun!

In 2010, Care-A-Van Ministries purchased a new mobile food pantry vehicle and the bus was remodeled to add additional seating in the back. In 2012, another truck was purchased to accommodate all of the ministry's cookout and band equipment. It continues to be used throughout the summers at Austin Park in Batavia for a public worship service and free picnic at which an average of more than three hundred meals are served each week.

By 2010 when I retired from my job at the New York State Education Department, Charlie was a well-established member of Care-A-Van's Monday morning prayer ministry, and I was happy to join the group. The "prayer bus" rotates between two locations on Main Street and one on Bank Street in Batavia each Monday morning, regardless of the weather, for a few hours of prayer, coffee or hot chocolate, and plenty of Christian encouragement.

Sometimes it's iron-sharpening time for the pastors and volunteers, while other times as many as a dozen additional souls will come aboard for prayer (or sometimes just a hot cup of coffee or to get out of the cold). Nobody leaves the bus without receiving an encouraging prayer.

Paul's motto is "We go even when the mailman doesn't go!" Many a weary traveler has been encouraged to stay the course and many a lively conversation has taken place as the iron slashes against the iron (Proverbs 27:17 NIV).

In addition to the morning prayer ministry and summer cookouts, Pastor Charlie served with Care-A-Van in the College Student Outreach Ministry, having paved the way for the ministry while he was the faculty leader of the Intervarsity Christian Fellowship group. We also occasionally helped out with Care-A-Van's Children's Halloween Outreach, providing cider, donuts, brownies, and hot chocolate, along with Christian tracts on Ellicott Street near Centennial Park, a highly traveled area for trick-or-treaters each year. We especially enjoyed delivering Christmas gifts, caroling with the Care-A-Van Christmas crew, and waving at the crowds from the bus during the seasonal parades.

Pastor Charlie always was the first to volunteer for the prayer tent at Caring for the City Day. Care-A-Van Ministries partners each year with a local dentist to offer free dental care (including cleanings, fillings, and extractions) for those who do not have dental insurance coverage. Many local agencies, ministries, and churches also join the event, offering free books, health care coverage information, cooking demonstrations, mammogram service information, smoke-free programs, free haircuts, and face painting for the children—and of course, they always received prayer and lots of encouragement from Pastor Charlie.

In 2011, Charlie was diagnosed with congestive heart failure. The doctor had prescribed a very strong diuretic, which Charlie vehemently opposed, quoting Revelation 22:2 and insisting that synthetic drugs were poison and that God certainly had provided a natural herbal cure that would work just as well—and certainly more safely.

Charlie was an avid listener to an Internet radio show that stressed the dangers of pharmaceuticals in favor of nutritional supplements, specialized magnets, herbs, and various other naturopathic remedies. He spent thousands of dollars on these alternative health remedies, labeling each with creative braille or voice labels. For example, psyllium was labeled, "Magic Poop Powder," and liquid silver was simply "Hi-Ho Silver!" I have saved many of the voice labels, accessed with a device called a Pen Friend, just to hear his voice.

In January 2012, Charlie required hernia surgery, while stubbornly continuing to fight the prescription diuretics for his congestive heart failure. Between his prideful refusal to take the medications and complications from the hernia surgery, he was in and out of the hospital until June 2012. Unable to keep anything down for three days straight, he was admitted to the hospital with congestive heart failure, renal failure, fever, and ascites with spontaneous bacterial peritonitis.

Following one of his physical therapy sessions in the hospital, Charlie was about to sit in the chair in his room when he stepped on something that punctured his foot. He told the therapist that he had stepped on something that was excruciatingly painful. The therapist looked at his foot and could find no puncture wound, looked around the chair, and told him that there was nothing there.

The following day, he complained again to the physical therapist of the pain in the arch of his foot, requesting Motrin. By the third day, the arch of his foot began to appear red and swollen, which we reported to his nursing staff. He continued to complain of increased pain in the foot, again requesting medication for the pain, and walking on the side of his foot to avoid weight bearing through the arch during therapy.

Charlie had had enough of the hospital. He wanted to go home. He'd had enough of doctors and medicines and certain individuals who refused to believe there was anything wrong with his foot. No matter how much I pointed out his injured foot to the hospital staff, they refused to acknowledge anything serious and couldn't convince Charlie to stay, so the hospital allowed him to be released. Nevertheless, he was back in the emergency room the very next day, asking for someone to find out what was in his foot. In spite of the red, swollen lump that was warm to the touch, they diagnosed plantar fasciitis and made an appointment four days later with a podiatrist.

By the time he arrived at the podiatrist, the nurse removed the bandage, took one look at the foot, and quickly ran for the doctor. The instant the doctor's scalpel touched Charlie's foot, it gushed and Charlie screamed. The doctor immediately called the emergency room to tell them he was sending Charlie for emergency surgery to remove the remainder of the infection under controlled conditions due to his congestive heart failure and diabetes.

Unfortunately, at that time the hospital had no clearly delineated procedure to ensure that the doctor's referral for emergency surgery was duly noted or even delivered to the emergency room doctor. Since Charlie's death, the hospital has instituted procedures requiring such communications to be electronically recorded in the patient's chart so that they are not misplaced or ignored.

The emergency room doctor admitted him to a room and placed him on IV antibiotics but without assigning any wound follow-up. Assuming the hospital had received the podiatrist's recommendation, I couldn't understand why no order was made for emergency surgery. I kept pleading with the nurses to have someone look at Charlie's foot, praying that the podiatrist's recommendations would eventually be heeded. Yet every time I went to the desk, they assured me that the antibiotics would take care of it and that a doctor would see him as soon as one was available.

All night, Charlie had increasing diarrhea and vomiting. The nurses couldn't keep up with Charlie and deal with any other patients, so I stayed to help him, all the while begging for someone to look at his infected foot, which in my spirit I felt was causing his illness.

At 12:30, Charlie seemed to be resting—we were both exhausted—so I went home. When I returned at 8:00 the next morning, I found Charlie hanging limp over the bed rail, having vomited all night long.

The nurse rushed in and said, "We've got to get some juice in him. His sugar is low."

I suspected that the juice would just come back up, so I suggested ginger ale. But he vomited that just as quickly. By 10:00, Charlie had become cold and clammy and his nurse had urgently called an ICU nurse to check in on him. His sugar was 23 and she couldn't get a blood pressure reading. He had become totally unresponsive—full code.

As lights and bells were going off and doctors and nurses scrambled to intubate and resuscitate Charlie, I screamed, running out of his room to a quiet corner of the hospital where I could get cell phone reception to call my prayer partner Eileen and ask her to pray with me. I desperately and tearfully prayed for peace and comfort so that I could be strong for Charlie.

I soon learned that he had gone into septic shock. Charlie was moved to the ICU and we were told that he had experienced multiple organ failure—including his heart, kidneys, and liver.

Because his kidneys did not respond within the critical time period, he needed to be transferred to another hospital where he could receive hemodialysis. The family chose to have him transferred to Buffalo, where he could be closer to his siblings in that area.

I learned that Charlie had suffered another heart attack upon arrival at Buffalo General. As soon as he was stabilized, the vascular surgical team rushed into the ICU.

They began operating right there in front of me in order to remove the infection from Charlie's foot. A local anesthetic may have injected infection deeper, and he was too unstable for general anesthetic, so no pain medication could be administered.

As Charlie writhed in pain, with a tube in his mouth and his hands tied to the bed rails, I watched them operate on his foot, removing infected tissue down to the tendons—while I prayed that he would not remember the pain and that this would save his life. They attached a wound vacuum. Charlie remained unresponsive.

Four days later, our prayers were answered. Charlie came out of the coma! In spite of the gravity of his circumstances, Charlie maintained his sense of humor as well as his loving concern for others. Thankfully, also in answer to prayer, he did not remember the pain from the emergency surgery on his foot.

He was later moved from the ICU to a private room and began receiving hemodialysis three days a week. Each night I would walk across the street to sleep at Kevin Guest House, the nation's first hospital hospitality house. I prayed that God would continue to heal my wondermous crepen.

Charlie especially delighted in being AWOL when I took him outside one afternoon. Down the elevator and out the front door, he rejoiced at feeling the warmth of the hot summer sun on his face and hearing the sounds of the traffic, sticking out his tongue at the thought that he was getting away with such a thing!

Because of the unique circumstances of Charlie's medical situation, with the exception of family members, we had very few visitors. This forced me to rely almost entirely on the Lord for comfort and strength throughout his hospitalization.

At the time, I didn't realize that Charlie was dying. If I had allowed myself to think about it logically, I should have known. He had gone into septic shock and all of his vital organs had shut down—including his liver, which was damaged beyond repair. We had all prayed when he went into the coma, and when he came out four days later, I praised God that He had given Charlie back to us.

His kidneys were gone so he required dialysis, but somehow the Lord allowed me to forget that the liver would not come back. He spent the majority of our twentieth wedding anniversary in dialysis, but he was alive!

God was so very present with us during Charlie's stay in the hospital. We were so very blessed to have a visit from one of Charlie's former Intervarsity Christian Fellowship students, as she happened to be in town on business with a company that actually designed the same type of catheters used for his dialysis!

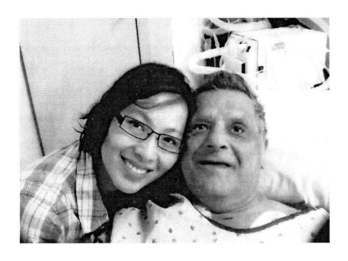

I was also blessed to be able to stay at Kevin Guest House instead of having to drive back and forth from our home in Batavia every day (a forty-five-minute drive each way). There were a few occasions in which the residents of the house exceeded the number of rooms, but I was especially blessed to be able to share a room with Karen and her nine-year-old daughter, with whom I had become friends.

Karen's husband had gone into septic shock; but fortunately his organs had rebounded and he did not require dialysis. However, due to the extensive therapy needed for him to regain the ability to walk, he remained in Buffalo even after Charlie was transferred to a rehabilitation facility.

This is the part that really amazes me about our loving God! The only facility that could deal with Charlie's wound vac *and* transport him to another town for dialysis three days per week just happened to be the very town where my new Kevin Guest House friends lived! The rehab center to which he was being sent was an hour-and-a-half drive from our home but just a few minutes from theirs.

Since she was still in Buffalo with her husband, this dear new friend graciously suggested that I could stay in her home—free of charge—so that I could spend every waking moment with Charlie! Karen understood that I was not only Charlie's wife and health care proxy, but because he was blind, I was also his eyes. I can never thank her enough for allowing me—a relative stranger—to stay in her home. The very idea is almost beyond my comprehension, but I praise God for her generosity!

I prayed that Charlie would recuperate and eventually come home. I never realized that instead he would soon be going home to be with the Lord.

It was a hot, dry summer, and about a week after Charlie was transferred to the rehabilitation center, I developed what I feared was strep throat. Thankfully, the culture came back negative. The clinic informed me that I probably had allergies, which I had never experienced before, nor have I since. Nonetheless, I was in a great deal of pain, both in my throat and my head due to the sinus congestion (not to mention the stress).

That Sunday, the rehabilitation center had a communion service. Since the person assigned to the worship music was sick, Charlie offered to accompany our singing on the piano.

Unfortunately, we soon discovered that the ammonia in his brain from the sepsis made it impossible for him to remember how to play the piano. However, everyone was gracious and thanked him anyway.

God had also graciously arranged that day for the center to have a family picnic, inviting the families of all the residents for hot dogs, hamburgers, baked beans, snow cones, and cotton candy. There was a bounce house for the little ones and a lady DJ playing Charlie's favorite kinds of music.

Charlie enjoyed being outside, eating the hot dogs and baked beans, and he bounced to the music as I wheeled his chair around in circles as if we were dancing. We told the DJ that we had not been able to celebrate our twentieth anniversary because he was in dialysis.

When she put on the next song, we knew that God had inspired it—the very first song we had danced to at our wedding reception: "Can I Have This Dance for the Rest of My Life?" by Ann Murray. That song was our first as well as our last dance—here on earth. Charlie passed away in his sleep that night, but God had given him the most beautiful last day on earth that He could, under the circumstances.

Yes, there is meaning behind the pain we bear; just as surely there is meaning behind Jesus's excruciating crucifixion and the Father's pain of turning His eyes away from His beloved Son when He bore our sins on the cross.

Just as the disciples were so close to Jesus that they couldn't understand why He had to die, we can't understand all the suffering we see on earth. Now we see through a glass, darkly, but when He returns, we will see Him face-to-face. Imagine the unspeakable joy of being face-to-face with Jesus!

Throughout his life, Charlie had occasionally been asked whether he would be willing to try out some of the experimental forms of artificial vision. He never hesitated to say, "The first thing I want to see is Jesus's face when He comes in the clouds to take me home!"

Listen, I tell you a mystery: We will not all sleep, but we will all be changed‐in a flash, in the twinkling of an eye, at the last trumpet. For the trumpet will sound, the dead will be raised imperishable, and we will be changed. For the perishable must clothe itself with the imperishable, and the mortal with immortality. When the perishable has been clothed with the imperishable, and the mortal with immortality, then the saying that is written will come true: "Death has been swallowed up in victory. Where, O death, is your victory? Where, O death, is your sting?" The sting of death is sin, and the power of sin is the law. But thanks be to God! He gives us the victory through our Lord Jesus Christ. Therefore, my dear brothers and sisters, stand firm. Let nothing move you. Always give yourselves fully to the work of the Lord, because you know that your labor in the Lord is not in vain.
—1 Corinthians 15:51–58 (NIV)

Brothers and sisters, we do not want you to be uninformed about those who sleep in death, so that you do not grieve like the rest of mankind, who have no hope. For we believe that Jesus died and rose again, and so we believe that God will bring with Jesus those who have fallen asleep in him. According to the Lord's word, we tell you that we who are still alive, who are left until the coming of the Lord, will certainly not precede those who have fallen asleep. For the Lord himself will come down from heaven, with a loud command, with the voice of the archangel and with the trumpet call of God, and the dead in Christ will rise first. After that, we who are still alive and are left will be

caught up together with them in the clouds to meet the Lord in the air. And so we will be with the Lord forever. Therefore encourage one another with these words.
—1 Thessalonians 4:13–18 (NIV)

For we walk by faith, not by sight. We are confident,
yes, well pleased rather to be absent from the
body and to be present with the Lord.
—2 Corinthians 5:6–8 (NKJV)

Obituary

Pastor Charlie Piscitello

BATAVIA — Pastor Charlie Piscitello, 69, of Batavia died peacefully Monday (July 30, 2012) at the Gowanda Rehabilitation and Nursing Center.

He was born in Buffalo Dec. 4, 1942, a son of the late Anthony and Anna (Gullo) Piscitello. Born with cataracts and glaucoma, and having several childhood accidents resulting in the eventual removal of both eyes, Charlie (then known as Chuck) attended the New York State School for the Blind. It was there on a coal pile that he found a guitar. Grounded to his room for being off limits, he taught himself to play the guitar, and later formed a band with several classmates and an instructor at the school. Charlie's first recordings of his music were made there on heavy vinyl disks. After leaving the school in 1961, Charlie formed his own band, playing various western New York venues.

Charlie later moved to the Southern Tier and hired a manager, John Perialas, with Pyramid Sound, based in Ithaca. He began touring more widely, eventually being in the "right place at the right time" to fill in for the Eagles, whose transportation failed to get them to their gig as the opening act for Blood, Sweat, and Tears. Charlie's music and charm impressed members of the band, who offered him a contract to continue the tour. With the stage name "Charlie Starr," Charlie cut several single 45-rpm recordings as well as two albums, entitled *Just Plain Charlie* and *Tough & Tender.*

Charlie's musical career spanned all 50 states, touring with individuals and groups which included the Moody Blues, James Taylor, Johnny Cash and the Carter family, Tina Turner, and the Carpenters, in addition to a tour of Europe with Yes. James Taylor graciously offered Charlie his song "One Man Dog" in reference to Charlie's guide dog, Princess, pictured on Charlie's "Just Plain Charlie" album cover.

Charlie rarely talked of his musical career in the later decades of his life, as his first love was Jesus. Abandoning fame and fortune to tune pianos and serve the Lord, Charlie left his musical career and dedicated his music and his life to the Lord.

In 1991, while living on a dairy farm in Greene, N.Y., Charlie met his wife, Judi. Not long after their marriage in 1992, Charlie began a small Bible study group in their home in Batavia.

While completing his associate's degree in counseling at Genesee Community College (GCC), Charlie worked at the Genesee Region Independent Living Center, and upon completion of his bachelor's degree from Empire State College in 1994, he was hired by GCC to work in its Center of Academic Progress. In 1997, he was ordained as a pastor by the Worldwide Church of God. Pastor Charlie founded the *Batavia Christian Fellowship*, which later became one with *Faith Community Chapel*. In 2002, he was among the first to be awarded the New York State Senate Achievers' Award by Senator Mary Lou Rath.

When his health began to fail, he was the pastor of *A Little House Church*. During the early years of his ministry, Pastor Charlie was a member of the Batavia Lions Club, volunteer for the Regional Action Phone, and the Salvation Army Disaster Team. More recently, Pastor Charlie was involved in the Monday morning prayer ministry of Care-A-Van Ministries, and occasionally joined the Care-A-Van Band, sharing the wonderful gospel of Jesus at every opportunity.

~

Precious in the sight of the Lord is the
death of His faithful saints.
—Psalm 116:15 (NIV)

As for you, go your way till the end. You will
rest, and then at the end of the days you will
rise to receive your allotted inheritance.
—Daniel 12:13 (NIV)

But those who hope in the Lord will renew their strength.
They will soar on wings like eagles; they will run and
not grow weary, they will walk and not be faint.
—Isaiah 40:31 (NIV)

So we are always confident, knowing that while we are at
home in the body we are absent from the Lord. For we walk by
faith, not by sight. We are confident, yes, well pleased rather
to be absent from the body and to be present with the Lord.
—2 Corinthians 5:6–8 (NKJV)

Afterwords

You love righteousness and hate wickedness; therefore God,
Your God, has set You above Your companions by anointing You
with the oil of joy. All Your robes are fragrant with myrrh and
aloes and cassia; from palaces adorned with ivory the music
of the strings makes You glad. Daughters of kings are among
Your honored women; at Your right hand is the royal bride
in gold of Ophir. Listen, daughter, and pay careful attention:
Forget your people and your father's house. Let The King be
enthralled by your beauty; honor Him, for He is your Lord!
—Psalm 45:7–11 (NIV)

After losing my precious Charlie, the pain was so deep that if I so much as looked at something that had belonged to him, I would be paralyzed with grief. My chest hurt as if an elephant were sitting on it. Even now, just the thought of Charlie seems to take my breath away, so Danny Gokey's song "Tell Your Heart to Beat Again" (https://www.youtube.com/watch?v=azYK8I2uoog), and the story behind it (https://www.youtube.com/watch?v=eUHRDCYnFfg), hold tremendous meaning for me. I even went to a heart specialist, but the stress test revealed no physical malady.

My emotions were raw and changed from moment to moment. My heart would stumble and careen from excruciating pain to despair, from anger to gut-wrenching sadness. I was tormented with questioning ("Why?" "What if ...?" "If only ..."), overwhelming fear and vulnerability, paralysis, numbness, and pure exhaustion.

Someone would show concern by asking, "How are you doing?"

How do I respond? Inside, I want to scream, "How in the world do you think I'm doing? I just lost the one I loved most in this world! My life is falling apart. There's no joy left on earth for me!

I don't even remember telling him that night how very much I loved him! He had wanted me to stay, but he wouldn't talk to me and my head was hurting so much that I went home.

Was he hurt that I had left him to die alone? Was he even aware that I had gone home? I hate being alone, and I don't know what God wants me to do with my life! I don't want to cook or eat. I just want to go to sleep and wake up from this nightmare!

Things that used to be fun because we did them together just bring back painful memories. He always did the household repairs and I don't have a clue! Why am I here?

Do people really want to know how I feel? My feelings don't stay put long enough for me to explain how I feel! All I can say is "Death stinks so life stinks! Charlie's death has killed me, too!"

Indeed, we felt we had received the sentence of
death. But this happened that we might not rely on
ourselves but on God, who raises the dead.
—2 Corinthians 1:9 (NIV)

Feeling as if the bottom had dropped out and fearing the crash after the free fall, I clung to the familiar routine of serving on the Care-A-Van Ministries prayer bus and summer picnic outreach. The church where Charlie's funeral was held became my home church. In addition, I attended other churches that met on Saturday nights or Sunday afternoons, needing to seek the Lord and Christian company as much as possible.

I was so paralyzed at first that I was afraid to linger on painful thoughts for fear they'd take me into a bottomless pit. So I let myself cry a bit so as not to deny my emotions completely, then pulled myself away to do something constructive. Certainly I mustn't grieve like those who have no hope (1 Thessalonians 4:13 NIV).

Thankfully since I was retired, I had been able to spend those precious last two years by Charlie's side. But now the light, wide-open schedule was weighing heavily upon my broken, lonely heart. I vividly remember my first worship service after Charlie's funeral. The praise team began singing "Blessed Be the Name of the Lord" and I gladly sang His praises, until the words of the chorus pierced my heart:

> He gives and takes away,
> He gives and takes away,
> My heart will choose to say,
> 'Blessed be the Name of The Lord!'

(Job 1:20 NIV), as the tears streamed down my face uncontrollably and I chose to raise my hands in worship of my True Husband (Revelation 21:2 NIV).

Because the summer was quickly coming to an end, I forced myself to start right away cleaning out some of the things that were of no use to me other than igniting searing, painful memories. I rented a small roll off and began with the garage (where Charlie had spent a majority of his summers). This wasn't easy, as every little tool was a tear trigger, but I forced myself to decide whether each item was trash, to be kept for my use, to be given to a family member, friend, or charity, or to be sold.

The process then progressed to Charlie's office (his winter retreat). Charlie had used his retirement savings to transform our covered patio into a beautiful, sun-filled office space with windows on three sides and used it both for his work from home for the college as well as for his work and counseling for the church.

With my emotions in pain and chaos, I needed to somehow create beauty and order as much as possible in my surroundings in order to balance out the inner turmoil. I needed to learn where the tools were located and reorganize things so that I could find them.

I also needed to return Charlie's office equipment to the college so that his office could be transformed from a painful memory into a welcoming sunroom.

I made a point to keep the bed made so that I wouldn't be tempted to hide there, and to keep the house clean and the curtains open to let in the sunshine. I even purchased fresh flowers for myself at home as well as for Charlie's grave for the first year or so, just for the bright colors and emotional uplift they provided in my darkened world.

My new pastor asked me to become the church clerk, working Tuesday and Thursday mornings to develop the weekly bulletin, keep up the church web site, and offer free coffee, prayer and encouragement to those in need.

I offered a women's Bible study in my home Tuesday nights and kept as busy as possible to avoid being alone with my pain, surrounded by things that triggered memories of Charlie.

I desperately looked to the Lord for comfort and for answers that only He could provide. In addition to attending church as often as possible, I immersed myself in prayer and in reading Scriptures and Christian books about death and heaven. I went to GriefShare meetings.

For a brief time, I seemed to have lost my identity. I was no longer a teacher, no longer a pastor's wife, no longer a wife, but who *am* I? I realized that I was no longer "Mrs." but was missing too much to be called "Miss."

I also realized from my knowledge of the Scriptures that Charlie would never again be my husband. ("At the resurrection people will neither marry nor be given in marriage; they will be like the angels in heaven," says Matthew 22:30 (NIV)). This only added to my grief.

I knew that as the bride of Christ, the church is betrothed to Jesus and will become one with Him at His return. I also believed that I would see Charlie then and thrilled at the thought that finally he would see me! Yet that thought soon evoked feelings of guilt that—if I was honest with myself—I was yearning to see Charlie even more than Jesus, my Creator, Lord, and Savior!

Drowning in conflicting doctrines and overcome with grief, I gasped and grasped out for a lifeline of hope. I longed to know what my beloved was doing "this very moment," when we would see one another again, and what it would be like.

I joined a support group for widows and widowers. The group is based upon the premise that those who are widowed are best able to support one another. Widowed folks uniquely understand the waves of emotions that widowhood washes over its victims, stealing away their breath, their identities, their joy, and sometimes even their hope—unless their hope is built upon the Rock of our salvation.

In an attempt to work through my grief, to regain my identity in Christ, and to honor Him and Charlie, I have written this book about the wonderful ways in which the Lord was lovingly weaving the intricate story line of Charlie's life. And I am thankful beyond words that He orchestrated it to intertwine—if only so briefly—with mine. My prayer is that Charlie's life story will continue to inspire others for many years to come.

The quotation that had been chosen for me in my high school yearbook was this: "Life, 'tis a glorious and happy thing." Jesus reminds us that the thief comes to steal, kill, and destroy, and that the last enemy to be destroyed is death (John 10:10, 1 Corinthians 15:26 NIV). The fear of death, grief over the death of a loved one, and death itself can steal our joy in life, if we let it. But Christ has come that we might have life to the full (John 10:10 NIV).

Jesus encourages each of us to step out in blind faith: to deny ourselves, take up the cross He has designed uniquely for us, and follow Him, even if we can only see "darkly." Jesus is the *only One* who can keep His promise never to leave or forsake us.

Nothing is right or fair in this life. The only thing that has held me together through this journey through the valley of the shadow of death has been my faith that this life is designed to teach us to love God first and others second. This world is not our home.

God designed families to teach us unconditional love—giving without expecting anything in return. If I expect this life to be fair, I will always be disappointed, but if I trust that God has much more for me when He returns if I learn to love Him first and others second, I have hope to go on through the pain.

Today I sing the praises of my Lord Jesus Christ, for He always keeps His promises! Although I bore no children, God blessed me on my wedding day with sweet grandchildren who are bringing forth great grandchildren to my heart's delight, for God knows that I have delighted myself in ministries to bring many more of His children to Him (Isaiah 54:1, Luke 1:45, Psalm 37:4 NIV).

It has been almost four years since Charlie's passing. Today would have been our twenty-fourth wedding anniversary. Anniversaries, birthdays, and holidays are always difficult. Our first anniversary after Charlie's death was excruciatingly painful; the second was painful with a touch of sweetness, and these past two years—remembering the sweetness with a touch of pain: the price of love. After all, the term *excruciating* originated with Jesus on the cross saying to us all, "I love you this much!"

The deeper our love, the deeper our pain. But just as the flowers are buried under the winter snows, I must remember that the sweetness of love is buried under all that pain. As the harsh cold and winter snows allow the flowers to rest, cleansing and refreshing the soil for new springtime blossoms and giving us time to appreciate all that winter takes away, this momentary separation from our loved ones deepens our love and appreciation for them and for all that Christ has given to us that we may have inadvertently taken for granted.

Jesus tells us that unless a kernel of wheat falls to the ground and dies, it remains only a single seed. But if it dies, it produces many seeds. The consolations of many endings are new beginnings. Jesus says, "Behold, I make all things new." Like a silversmith melts the silver in the fire in order to strain away the dross, Jesus allows us to endure fiery trials to develop our faith and strength in Him, until He can see His image in us. As we die daily to our own desires and focus on fulfilling God's will, others see less of us and more of Him.

I am now able to wear one of Charlie's shirts without falling into a heap on the floor. I just cuddle up in it and smile. Our threefold cord (Ecclesiastes 4:12) was temporarily unraveled but not broken. As I cling to Christ all the more tightly, He will hold me close until He returns to unite us all in His kingdom!

I have learned that it's not our families or our belongings, our abilities or disabilities, or our careers or anything else in this world that defines us. It is our relationship with Jesus Christ that gives us our true identity. He has given each of us a unique purpose in His overall plan for His eternal family. He gave us each special gifts and circumstances and people with whom to share. He purchased us with His life, and we belong to Him. He is our Creator and our God and we are His people, His church, His bride. We must sanctify ourselves in order to be ready for His return (Revelation 19:7)!

Second Corinthians 5:7 certainly applied to Charlie, as he truly learned to walk by faith, not by sight. Although there was no light in his plastic eyes, there was much light in his life. Charlie's headstone, quoting John 9:25, says, "I was blind but now I see." True faith sees beyond the grave.

So many Scriptures have taken on different and much deeper meaning for me since Charlie first went into the hospital. God's Word is *alive* to comfort, nourish, and sustain us and to give us hope and a future worth seeking out according to His loving will!

Each person's journey with Jesus is unique. However, there are common emotions to which others can relate—even if our circumstances are different and even when our feelings are painful beyond description. Through death, we learn to value the sacredness of every life.

I have tried to look back as objectively as possible upon my "wondermous" life with Charlie. Although Charlie was far from perfect, God knew that he and I would be good for one another in bringing about His plan for our lives.

If I had not lost Charlie, I would not have realized that my love for him had all too often tipped the scales dangerously toward idolizing him. There is no other god but the Lord Jesus. He is the only One whose unconditional love never fails, because we can't give Him anything that He hasn't already given to us first. He is the giver of life and His banner over us is love (Song of Songs 2:4 NIV).

I now understand much better why Charlie rarely talked about his musical career. Charlie Starr had been crucified with Christ and Charlie Piscitello had become a new creation, humbling himself before his Lord (Galatians 2:20; 2 Corinthians 5:17 NIV). Charlie adamantly preferred to be remembered as a pastor, even going as far as wearing a clerical collar with his Romans 1:16 T-shirt his final day on earth.

One of the handmade cards Charlie had sent while we were dating reads,

> To you I pledge my love forever. To you I will give myself completely. Our love is from God. Our love is the Christ in us. Together we can make it through eternity. With God, nothing is impossible (Matthew 19:26; Mark 10:27).

The old cliché "You don't know what you've got until you lose it" may be true, but—praise Jesus—I haven't lost Charlie at all!

The Lord has shown me that the qualities I had loved most about Charlie were those that best reflected Jesus. It was Christ living in Charlie that I have cherished all along!

In Charlie's death, I have learned to trust so much more in the One who created us, the One who loves us, the One who died for our sins so that we can be one with Him forever: Jesus! I believe that our family relationships here on earth are designed by God to give us just an appetizer—a tiny foretaste of the exquisite joy we will experience in our oneness at the wedding supper of the Lamb when Christ returns for His bride (John 17:20–23; Ephesians 5:21–33; Colossians 1:27)!

When my Charlie took his last breath almost four years ago, I felt as if my own breath had been taken as well. Keeping busy became my anesthetic of choice. But I still couldn't breathe until I gave myself the Sabbath margin to allow myself the time and space to look to the Giver of life and breath. When you can't see the forest for the trees—focusing either on the pain or the "shiny things" of the present—you need to rise above them to obtain His eternal perspective. I am learning to take one day, one hour, and one moment at a time, to cherish the memories, and to accept the "present" as the gift that it is.

If I had not experienced the stabbing pain of sin, I would never have appreciated God's mercy, forgiveness, and salvation. If I had not tasted the bitter tears of grief, I would never have appreciated the amazing grace, hope, and joy of the resurrection of all who sleep in Him (1 Thessalonians 4:13 NIV)!

In her book, *Children of the Day*, Beth Moore likens a Christian's tears to "liquid language set to the tune of the Holy Spirit's groanings (Romans 8:26)." Beth goes on to say, "The wounds of Christ are never more sacred to us than when we feel the stab of this fallen world's blade and hasten to Him ... To the degree we have loved, we often mourn; but we can be whole again piece by piece if we accept what 1 Thessalonians 4:13 holds in its other hand."

I am part of the bride of Christ. Therefore, Christ Himself is my Beloved Husband and my hope! Jesus loves us all unconditionally. He has walked with us through our sin and sadness. He poured out His blood to cover our sins. A Man of sorrows, He has felt our overwhelming grief. By bearing the full weight of the sins of the world—yet Himself without sin—He alone has conquered both sin and its ultimate penalty: death!

Jesus has promised never to leave or forsake us, and His name is Emmanuel, which means "God with us." Jesus is always in the garden, yearning to walk and talk with us. Hallelujah!

Brothers and sisters, we do not want you to be uninformed about those who sleep in death, so that you do not grieve like the rest of mankind, who have no hope. For we believe that Jesus died and rose again, and so we believe that God will bring with Jesus those who have fallen asleep in Him. According to the Lord's word, we tell you that we who are still alive, who are left until the coming of the Lord, will certainly not precede those who have fallen asleep. For the Lord Himself will come down from heaven, with a loud command, with the voice of the archangel and with the trumpet call of God, and the dead in Christ will rise first. After that, we who are still alive and are left will be caught up together with them in the clouds to meet the Lord in the air. And so we will be with the Lord forever. Therefore encourage one another with these words!
—1 Thessalonians 4:13–18 (NIV)

CPSIA information can be obtained
at www.ICGtesting.com
Printed in the USA
FSOW01n1635271116
27784FS